clean&simple

SCRAPBOOKING | THE SEQUEL

clean&simple

SCRAPBOOKING | THE SEQUEL

BY CATHY ZIELSKE

SIMPLE SCRAPBOOKS

Founding Editor
Stacy Julian

Editor in Chief
Lin Sorenson

Special Projects Editor
Lynda Angelastro

Copyeditor
Kelley J. P. Lindberg

Editorial Assistant
Carolyn Jolley

Creative Director
Cathy Zielske

Photography
Timothy Boothby, Symoni Johnson, Tara Whitney

PRIMEDIA

VP, Group Publisher
David O'Neil

SVP, Group Publishing Director
Scott Wagner

Senior Product Manager
Dana Wilson

For information on carrying *Simple Scrapbooks* products in your retail store, please call (800) 815-3583. For information on ordering *Simple Scrapbooks* magazine, call toll-free (866) 334-8149. *Simple Scrapbooks* is located at 14850 Pony Express Road, Bluffdale, Utah, 84065. Phone: (801) 984-2070.

Home page: simplescrapbooksmag.com

Printed in Korea

ISBN 1-933516-19-4

THIS BOOK WILL NOT:

clean your house

show you how to get 14 photos or more on a layout

help your children to listen better

explain heat embossing in excruciating detail

solve a single world problem

make you a better cook

answer all of your most pressing life questions

THIS BOOK WILL:

make you feel really good about yourself

remind you of why you scrapbook

encourage you to put off the laundry for a few more minutes

help you to refine your skills of observation

cause you to shout, "Hey, I do that, too!"

show you the critical difference between "should do" and "could do"

remind you of something that by now, I think you already know:

scrapbooking is cool.

FINE PRINT:

No one should have to enter scrapbooking therapy after reading this book.
This is my approach. Scrapbooking, much like life, is not one size fits all.

contents

104

make

Want to see a cute simple theme album? And another? And one more? What? How do you make one? Well, it just so happens, I have an entire chapter to answer that very question.

134

enjoy

A compendium of style, creativity and organization. It's also the final chapter of this book. If that thought makes you sad, you can always start again from the beginning, okay?

clean and simple, part deux

It's been nearly two years since I wrote *Clean & Simple Scrapbooking*, and I'll be perfectly honest: I had no intention of doing another book about the same old stuff. Nope. Not me. I wanted to break new ground, explore new scrap worlds and become the all-new-and-improved Cathy Z.

But a funny thing happened during the process. As I started writing, I realized that the original ideas behind the first book still guided me in my journey as a scrapbooker. Keeping it simple. Telling good stories. Designing attractive pages. And having fun. Why on earth would I want to change that?

Now I don't know if that's taking the easy way out, or just realizing that at its core, this hobby is very simple. Take a photo. Tell a story. Save a memory. There's no rule that says, "Thou shalt reinvent wheel." What worked for me then continues to work for me now.

Here's something I *am* quite certain of: my hobby makes me pay attention to my life. Seemingly inconsequential things can spawn entire albums. Life has little bits of magic at nearly every turn, if you're looking closely enough. Scrapbooking has refined my senses. It's made me hungry to use it before I lose it. It's made me remember that I don't remember what it was like to be nine years old. And that I will never live in a Pottery Barn house. And that as tiny as I am in the scope of the universe, no one lives a life like mine. Not even the people whose meals I cook, whose laundry I fold, and whose cheeks I kiss at night.

I am a scrapbooker. I'm not embarrassed to say that. Not anymore. Not when I've met so many amazing people, and heard so many moving stories, and seen how powerful a little paper and glue can be, when combined with photos, memories—and above all—our voices.

We find our voices through scrapbooking. That might not be what we set out to do, but somehow…it's inevitable. You can only do so many birthday layouts before that voice within starts coming out to play.

Then look out. Your voice is growing and getting stronger. The universe has no choice but to listen.

So here's to detail. To things both large and small. To stories, photos, paper and glue. To not reinventing the wheel, but to rotating the tires once in a while, and always enjoying the ride.

I hope you know how the memories you record are affecting and enhancing lives.

Especially yours.

Cathy

For Dan. My soul mate. My friend. My shining reminder of manly goodness. You save my life on a daily basis. You let me be me. It's like winning the lottery. For Aidan and Cole. For giving me this ride called motherhood. I love the two of you beyond sane reason. For my parents, Murray and Shirley. For giving me all the stuff I needed to turn into a pretty alright person. Thank you. For Molly, just because. For Tara, Donna, Margie, Lisa, Suz and Shelley. For helping me to stay sane and giving me a social network. For Stacy, for just being Stacy. And Lin, for mid-morning phone calls. For the smart folks at Apple Computer, for making such great computers that let me do what I do for a living. For the Taste of India restaurant in Maplewood. For music by Foo Fighters and Green Day. For the makers of Flavorice. For cool fronts in August. For Pick-a-Size paper towels. For Aveda hair products. For anyone who I've ever met over the entire span of my 39 years of living, and was nice to me. Thank you.

dedicated with love and gratitude

d

how to use this book

Open it and read it. I'm serious!

This book is divided into five chapters. And everything in those chapters is broken up into nice little digestible chunks of scrapbooking goodness. If you're a page flipper (and you know who you are) then I urge you to get the flipping out of the way first, and come back to the text at a later time.

Why? Because I've got lots to say, and share, and ramble on about. And it's not just rambling for rambling's sake; it's with the hope that you'll say, "A-ha! I get it!" That's ultimately the goal of this book.

Use this book for ideas. Scraplift pages. Adapt. Re-interpret. But above all, use it to remember why it is you do what you do: scrapbook.

This book focuses on some basic philosophies of scrapbooking the simple way: have more fun, let go of unrealistic expectations, capture the essence of what matters most, and—did I mention have more fun?

I don't expect you to start scrapbooking like me. This book isn't about telling you how to scrapbook; it's about sharing ideas and stories and information to inspire you to become more of the scrapbooker you are.

What you will find in the following pages are a lot of basic things about this hobby. When I was writing this book, I kept thinking, "Hmmm…I'm not really breaking any new ground here." And then it hit me: bingo! That's ridiculously okay! The things that will make you a better scrapbooker are the cornerstones: solid design and real stories. Good photos are a bonus, but in the end, not as important as the memories you're saving.

So sit back (when you have a spare moment from work, kids, spouse, mail, e-mail, phone calls, and any other modern day duty that keeps you from sitting back), and spend a little time with me.

Let's have some fun, talk about scrapbooking, and feel the love. Deal? Deal.

I scrap

create

WONDER

explore (ek·splor) 1. to investigate and examine something carefully 2. travel in a little known region 3. to search and seek out

keep life simple

·live·

celebrate

shop

AM

think

Do you think about scrapbooking? I mean really, really think
about it. About the whys, the whats, and the what ifs? To me,
this hobby is more than just photos. It's more than paper flowers
and mini-brads. And it's so much more than beautiful, completed
albums all in a row. It's simply life, preserved with a little bit
of adhesive and a whole lot of heart. Don't you think that's
a nice way to put it? Let's discuss. And...think.

what is it that you do, anyway?

I'm always surprised at the reactions I get from people when I tell them what I do with so much of my spare time. But I can never just say, "scrapbooking," and leave it at that. I feel this moral obligation to elaborate—to help vaporize the stereotype of ladies wearing applique sweaters, running amok with decorative scissors and teddy bear stickers.

See, the scrapbooking of today is really an exploration of life through words and images. It gives people the chance to celebrate that which matters, that which enlightens, that which makes up the very fabric of life. It's really cool. No, I'm serious. I see you smirking, but I'm telling you: don't knock it until you try it, and then, don't come crying to me when you've maxed out your credit cards on scrapbook stuff.

I scrapbook because it makes me a better person, and I want to leave better than I came.

STACY JULIAN

So what's your answer when people ask you? Do you ramble? Do you tell them it's a subculture of people who are slowing down and taking notice of the details? Do you tell them new cardstock colors make you giddy? Do you tell them it's not just about kids' birthdays and dance recitals and Christmas? Do you tell them you are simply saving the memorable bits and pieces of your life?

Me? I say all of the above. And by that time they've either walked away or we're in the car, headed to the nearest scrapbook store.

textured cardstock   the colors pink, brown and green

repositionable adhesive   paper flowers   mini-brads

rub-ons   getting the story just right   playing

getting new binders in fun colors   coming up with titles

coming across that single photo that takes your breath away

foam tape   the colors orange and blue   mini glue dots

oversized letter stickers   discovering cool storage options

ribbon—even though I don't use it that much—i still love it

purging old products   buying new   ordering cardstock

fresh Xacto blades for my knife   the people I get to meet

documenting the every day kind of stuff that makes up my life

the freedom to be authentic and create   making mini albums

this is the stuff about scrapbooking that just makes me happy

art

happy

COME ON, GET HAPPY

When was the last time you created a page about why you scrapbook? Or why it makes you happy? Try it. You'll like it. Plus, it's a shameless excuse to use the new product you just dropped $30 on at the scrapbook store.

A few weeks ago, I stumbled across this quote while reading my buddy Ali's blog. She'd said it "struck a chord" with her. For me, it struck an entire symphony. I quickly copied and pasted it into a blank Quark document, to revisit at another time. I knew, deep down, I'd read something that would inspire me down the road.

The more I thought about the quote, the more I realized, with extreme clarity: "This is it!" *This* was the reason why I did this nutty scrapbooking thing. *I was here. I was hungry. I was sad. I existed!*

That *is* what it's all about, really. Rather than getting bogged down by the little details, I'm uplifted by them on a daily basis. And I record them on my scrapbook pages.

It's funny…I don't think of myself as an "artist." Never have, really. What I *am*, however, is a reporter; an observer; a documentary–maker about the world that is constantly spinning around me, making me who I am and showing me what life is, in all its glorious detail.

What I *am* is a creator. I think it's an innately female thing, to create. And it's a natural extension of that very female nature to give "birth" to a record of our lives.

"Above all else, it is I was here. I was hungry. I was defea love. I was afraid. I was hopeful. I had and that's why I made works of art."

OUTTAKES

about leaving a mark that I existed:
ted. I was happy. I was sad. I was in
an idea and I had a good purpose

—Felix Gonzalez-Torres

ended family
dan photos
athy photos
everyday life
places we go
aidan photos
favorite photos

And behind it all is good purpose. I think that's a metaphor for my life. Whether I succeed wildly, or fail with a flourish, my intentions as a human being are always good.

I have good intentions when I share and remember and reflect and project, even when the outcome may not be that fabulous, or even remotely desired. This is true both in life, and on my scrapbook pages.

But it's those very pages that afford me the opportunity to celebrate what really matters—to discover who I am and will continue to become in the scheme of my life.

I think that's what art is all about, and therefore, scrapbooking qualifies as much as any other discipline. For like all art, there is a certain, undeniable measure of heart that goes into each and every piece. And that is the kind of emotion I try my best to capture and convey.

I've said it before: it is so much more than paper and glue. It's not about slapping down photos and calling it a day.

I existed. I had an idea and I had good purpose. This is why I do what I do.

MAR 0 7 2005

for the love of cardstock

I won't deny the joy I feel when acquiring new scrapbooking "stuff." New Making Memories? Gotta have it. New Chatterbox? Bring it on. New KI Memories? Here's my credit card.

But for people starting out, it can be a bit overwhelming. The good news? Truthfully, you don't need much more than photos and cardstock to make a great scrapbook page. Even with my obscene stash of supplies, I often have to force myself to use more than just cardstock, pictures and words. I like the pure simplicity of cardstock. Something about it says, "My story and photos can stand on their own." It reminds me that ultimately, a story is a story; the dressing up part is really secondary.

Cardstock-only layouts are underrated. Sure, I love adding a tiny embellishment here and there, but if you've got cardstock, adhesive, photos and words, you honestly don't need anything else to muck it up.

You don't need to find a guitar sticker to do a page about your kid rocking out to music he probably isn't even old enough to listen to. Just pick some cool cardstock colors. And be done.

Cardstock—like my son—rocks.

GREEN DAY

My boy rocks. Literally. There was a Green Day concert on AOLmusic.com, and Cole grabbed his hockey stick/guitar, microphone/pen and proceeded to rock out to the entire *American Idiot* album. Sure, there's a few bad words every now and then. But we live in a free country, and I believe there really is a place for well-placed profanity. Never mind the fact that this Green Day album is probably one of the best albums, beginning to end, to come out in years. So maybe I have to turn the volume down on certain parts. I have to say, he's got good taste for a six year old. And you never know. This scrapbook page might one day show up on a future edition of **VH1 Behind the Music.** *Influenced early on by bands like Green Day, Coleman eventually put down the hockey stick and picked up a used Fender at the age of six...You never know.* OCTOBER 2005

eggs-hilaration

1. the magical effect of transforming Easter eggs; 2. the magical effect on Mom seeing the two of you co-exist peacefully.

CARDSTOCK RULES

I love nothing more than creating a simple page using only cardstock, and maybe a font or two. This design is simple and do-able, and it tells a quick, visual story with little fanfare. Don't feel like you have to pull out all the stops when creating a layout. Sometimes, cardstock alone will do just fine.

size doesn't matter, go figure

I, Cathy Zielske, being of relatively sound mind and body, and a die-hard 8½ x 11 scrapbook afficionado, can make 12 x 12 pages. Who knew?

It all started when I picked up a copy of what has become one of my all-time favorite idea books: *A Designer's Eye for Scrapbooking*, by Ali Edwards. As I poured over Ali's pages, admiring the strength of her voice and her linear, graphic approach to design, it suddenly hit me: Hey, she makes 12 x 12 pages. And they look really clean and simple. Maybe I can do this too!

So I pulled out a sheet of 12 x 12 cardstock, opened Ali's book for inspiration, and created the scrapbook page you see on the facing page.

As one who uses the computer to create the majority of my journaling and titles, the only hurdle I faced was how to print them on 12 x 12 paper. My regular format printer was not going to accept a sheet of that size. Then I remembered: I'm a scrapbooker. I can piece things together to make a finished page.

Since that time, I've been mixing it up, size-wise. I'm learning that there are times when a 12 x 12 page is a better canvas for a particular story and set of photos. So if you're scratching your head and wondering if you're seeing things, rest assured, you're not. I've rejoined the 12 x 12 sisterhood. Size just doesn't matter anymore.

WHO KNEW?

No one says you have to lock into a single size when scrapbooking. Whether it's 12 x 12, 8 x 8, or 6 x 6, the size you choose is totally up to you. Scrapbooking should be flexible enough to fit the stories and memories you're saving. And guess what? It is.

take me out

KANSAS CITY T-BONES	
PRIETO	CF
M. BROWN	2B
R. BROWN	1B
PEARSON	DH
NOWLIN	LF
JONES	3B
SOSEBEE	RF
CERIANI	C
HILL	SS

0 for 1   LAST AT BAT
GROUND OUT
MPH   BALL   STRIKE   OUT

...to the ball game. Take me out to the crowds. Actually, the best part about having season tickets to the St. Paul Saints? Me, getting three hours to myself on any given home game night all summer long. Oh sure, I go maybe once or twice a season, but really, it's a dad and kids thing. A cool tradition. Baseball outside, with all the goofy side shows. As it should be. Me? I can use those three hours to sleep, scrapbook, watch mindless television, do laundry, clean the house, sleep some more, or, just stare off into space and enjoy the silence. Until the phone rings, and I get the mandate: "Game's over. Come get us!" And then I drive the less than two miles to the ball park. Refreshed. Ready to go. I say bring on the summer Northern League season. It spells one nice three-hour break for mom. Buy me some peanuts and mental health. I take all that I can get. 8.05

Mom …it's a name I go by in this house, but I have to be completely honest: there are days when the sound of it rings just a bit too shrilly in my ears. Today is one of those days. Don't get me wrong. I hate to be sounding anything but thankful these days—thankful for my life, my family, my friends, my work—but still, the word sometimes rubs me the wrong way. | It's all about tone, really. There is a certain *"Mom!"* that you know is either going to involve some sort of minor injury or other catastrophic social event (i.e. sibling fights). Then it's going to be Mom's role to figure it all out. Or, there's the other *"Mom!"* that is sure to be followed with request, after request, after request. | I'm not superhuman. I am, as I love to say, just as God made me, sir. Maybe it was the lingering aftermath of the root canal I had at 8 o'clock this morning. Maybe it was the four hours of computer hades and holding on the line for support technicians. Maybe it was that every now and then, I just get a little bit tired of being "Mom." | I know it's the introvert in me. That sometimes, I need to curl up, and drift away for a bit. That's how I return to the living sane. And then, once I'm back, well baby, bring it on. Until the sound of *"Mom"* sends me off to write yet another journaling block about how sometimes, I've heard the word one too many times…again.

BUT WHERE DOES IT ALL GO?

Once I started making 12 x 12 pages, I had to figure out where to put them. Did I have to start buying 12 x 12 albums for every person in my family? Did I have the space on my shelves for such a monster size?

My answers are "No" and "Sort of." I've picked up a couple of 12 x 12 binders to store my pages in for now. I'll worry about rhyme and reason later. (To see how I organize the rest of my pages, see p. 150.)

have pen, will write

I did it. I finally got over my fear of using my own handwriting on my scrapbook pages. For a control freak like me, this was no small feat.

I was plagued by the "but my handwriting will ruin the scrapbook page" syndrome. What? You suffer from it, too? Well, if a die-hard computer journaler like me can see the light at the tip of a pen, anyone can.

Truth be told, I got tired of running upstairs to my computer to type out my journaling. I wanted to stay in one place while scrapping. Also, I wanted to break the chains of feeling like my handwriting was a big pile of *ka-ka du jour*.

My scrapbook friends were using their handwriting. Sure, they had more whimsy in a single cursive letter than I had in a whole alphabet, but if they could do it, why not me? The other issue at hand was this: would it hold up to my own need for visual order? Part of the joy I feel in scrapbooking is creating something that, when finished, I like to look at. If I was forcing the handwriting issue, and it was not making me happy, I knew I'd have to give it up.

But one night, I was scrapping at my friend Vicky's house, and I did the "Pink" layout on the facing page. And something just clicked. I felt like running down the streets of Champlain, Minn., screaming, "I used my handwriting and I like it!"

It was so liberating. Now, I use my handwriting more and more. I've found that it alters the style of my pages. I use more stamp inks to add dimension to elements. I use sandpaper to shabby things up a bit. I like to call my foray into hand-written pages "Cathy Z., Part Deux" (see sidebar, next page).

But you know what? I still manage to preserve the linear foundation of my pages, and it's made me realize that I can have it both ways. It's been an absolute eye opener for me—that being, "Hey, my handwriting doesn't suck nearly as bad as I thought it did."

I DON'T SEEM TO REALLY WEAR IT, OR FILL MY HOUSE WITH THINGS IN THIS HUE, OR PAINT MY WALLS WITH IT, BUT WHEN IT COMES TO SCRAP-RELATED THINGS, PINK IS WHERE ITS AT, BABY. ITS THE GO-TO COLOR. ITS DA BOMB, AS THE KIDS IN 1996 MIGHT HAVE SAID. ITS ALSO MY SECOND FAVORITE COLOR. (NEXT TO LIME/CHARTREUSE GREEN, OF COURSE) PINK... ITS FRESH. IT GOES SO WELL WITH BLACK & WHITE PHOTOS. AND BROWN. AND ORANGE. AND GREEN. AND WITH ITSELF. ITS BUBBLE GUM AND COTTON CANDY, WHICH MEANS THERES AN UNDERLYING INNOCENCE, AND THAT MUST BE A DEEP-SEATED DESIRE IN ME TO BE MORE PINK AS A PERSON. SO YOU MIGHT NOT FIND ME IN A PINK JUMPSUIT, SKIPPING THROUGH THE STREETS OF ST. PAUL, IT DOESN'T MEAN THAT I AM NOT PINK TO THE CORE. SO THIS IS MY TRIBUTE TO PINK, MMMMMMMMM.

Love Cathy

4.15.05

PINK

my second favorite color

happy

love

CHANNELING MY INNER SWAPP

I find myself at a stylistic crossroads every time I use my own handwriting. Somehow, it feels like things need to be a little rougher, a little more organic. Don't get me wrong; I'm not going to do anything rash like tilting a photo on a layout. But I do feel like being a little more random and artistic. I call it "channeling my inner Swapp." It's my attempt to be more funky, like the inspiring scrapbook artist Heidi Swapp.

So Heidi, if you're out there, thanks for helping me get over myself. See those foam stamps on the "Torture" layout to the left? Heidi gave them to me at a scrapbook show and said, "You'd better use them!" I did, along with some paint and my own handwriting. Go me!

coffee in duluth, the morning

AFTER MY BIG, GARGANTUAN MELTDOWN. A LITTLE EXPLANATION... DAN HAD PLANNED A SURPRISE WEEKEND GET-AWAY TO DULUTH. NOW I WAS NEVER REALLY ONE TO ROLL WITH PUNCHES, BUT AFTER BEING ASSURED THAT OUR DOG WOULD BE ABLY CARED FOR WHILE WE WERE AWAY, I DECIDED TO TRY TO ENJOY THE SPONTANEITY OF IT ALL. THAT WAS UNTIL WE GOT THERE, AND I CALLED HOME TO CHECK ON DYLAN, AND MAKE SURE SHE'D HAD HER MEDICATIONS. THERE WAS NO ANSWER. SO, I CALLED AGAIN. AND AGAIN, AND AGAIN. YOU GUESSED IT— NOBODY HOME. SO I PROCEEDED TO FREAK OUT, CERTAIN DYLAN WAS ALONE & HAVING SEIZURES. FINALLY, AT AROUND 11 P.M., SOMEONE WAS HOME. ALL WAS FINE. OUR HOUSE SITTER HAD JUST GONE OUT FOR A BIT. BUT STILL, I'D MADE A MAJOR DENT IN OUR WEEKEND FUN. WHEN I LOOK AT THIS PHOTO, I'M AWARE OF THE PROGRESS I'VE MADE TOWARDS BECOMING A SLIGHTLY CALMER PERSON.

JOURNALING ON AUGUST 14, 2005

YOU'VE COME A LONG WAY, BABE!

DO THIS NOW!

Put this book down. (Well, finish reading this part first, then you can put it down.) Go find a photo you've been wanting to scrapbook. Make a layout and hand-write the journaling. If you hate it, crumple it up, throw it away and laugh maniacally while you do it. Or, if—gasp—you like it, do a celebratory dance. Either way, at least you can say, "Hey, I tried it!" Go you!

It's amazingly simple to use handwriting. When I'm writing by hand, I just design the page and write in the space left over for journaling. If I run out of room, it's no big deal. I end my sentence, and voila, the page is done.

Handwriting feels organic and true. Almost more "scrapbooky" to me. And I like that. It doesn't mean that I'm going to ditch fonts and use only handwriting. It just means that I've made peace with my scrawl and given it a home in the pages of my scrapbooks.

THE PEN IS YOUR FRIEND

If I can do it, so can you. Here are some ways to get more comfy with your handwriting:

- **Buy a blank notebook and just practice writing.** Experiment with different types of pens and pencils. Write big, write small, write in cursive, write in capital letters. Get used to your writing. Just write like you. Don't feel you have to imitate anyone.

- **Pencil in your journaling first.** Then you can be sure it looks okay before you commit it to ink. I tried this in the beginning, but quickly realized that it was defeating my purpose of using my own handwriting. (That purpose being FREEDOM!) Now, I just grab the pen and write. If I mess up, big stinkin' deal!

- **Relax.** Don't stress about your handwriting. If you really don't like it, then create a layout with hidden journaling, or tuck the journaling into a library pocket and call it a day.

sweeping versus specific

Events or moments? Moments or events? What type of page do you create most? And, why is there a debate over the value of one over the other?

My friend and colleague, Stacy Julian, said it best in her book, "The Big Picture." She wrote, "Both events and moments are really about the people experiencing them. Scrapbook *people*."

Can I get a hallelujah from the choir? In the end, we scrapbook about people. And the places they go. And the things they do. Whether it occurs within the moment, or across a span of time that comprises an event, it's still just a record of life.

I'm doing away with the "event" and "moment" terminology. For me, it's now become "sweeping"

or "specific." The layout below is "sweeping"— it relates a wide-angle view of a particular event (a family camping trip) in my life. However, the layout on the facing page is "specific"—it magnifies one moment or idea within the overall event (my daughter's two cousins and their relationship).

I prefer specific over sweeping. I prefer the little details over the broad brush strokes. More life can be found in the little parts. More personality. More of what makes the people who they are, or the places what they mean, or the things that they represent. Plus, it takes a lot more time and thought to put 12 photos on a layout. If I need to use that many photographs, my photo albums start to look mighty appealing.

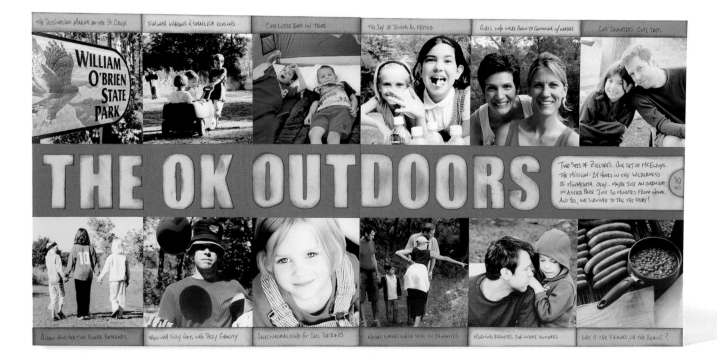

{ Rachael&Micah }

Whether it's on a 24-hour camping trip in the quasi-Minnesota wilderness, or just hanging out for the day in the basement of our house, Rachael and Micah are Aidan's blonde bookends. Where Aidan goes, you're sure to find one little Zielske cousin on either side.

August 2005

bookends

UP WITH PEOPLE!

Specific pages really just celebrate the details. Relationships, moments, experiences. This layout is technically a "moments" page. But remember, it's simply a more detailed exploration of the people involved. Specific doesn't have to mean exhaustive journaling either. It just means a single, specific subject, isolated and magnified or expounded upon.

I realize that a lot of scrapbookers want sweeping, and I say, if that's what makes you happy, then by all means, sweep away. However, don't let the details you *could* capture get swept under the "We had a really great time and here are 14 pictures to prove it" rug. Because eventually that rug of memory will fade without the details, and a bunch of pretty pictures will be missing their story.

Nine times out of ten, I'm taking the specific approach. I'm happy using one photo on a page, if it means I'm able to use the remaining space to tell a complete, detailed story.

If you are a scrapbooker who likes sweeping layouts, start a new trend: a sweeping approach, with very specific details in the journaling.

I CAN'T WORK THAT HARD

While making this page, I realized that scrapping all those photos made me think way too hard. I want to feel creative and have fun while scrapbooking, not like I'm solving an intricate puzzle. The page on the right took me half the time to finish, took place during the same event, contains the same general info about the fair, and yet focuses on a specific "thing" I wanted to document.

My goal with scrapbooking is to tell stories. Photos are just one part of that process. And you have to admit, my candid shots of our day at the fair are less than stellar. Note to self: put those in the photo album and scrap the stories that matter most to you. I can do that? Really? Oh, good. Thanks.

Eight hours. Garlic fries. Snow cones. Fried green tomatoes. Animal smells. Lots of overpriced rides. And tired kids. Ah, must be our annual visit to the Minnesota State Fair. Tired kids, or kid, I should say, indeed. Cole was about two hours into our adventure when he began the "Carry me" chant. I kept telling him, "Well honey, if you're too tired to walk after just a few hours, maybe we need to take you to a doctor!" That line never works. He just knew he wanted to be carried. I had Dan take this picture (because I rarely, if ever make appearances in photos with the family) and even though I have my shades on, and Cole's not even close to looking into the camera, it sort of melts my heart and makes me just a titch sad. In all my complaining about piggy backs during the fair, and trading off with Dan, I can't deny this one fact: I won't be slinging him around much longer. Aidan, at nine, is to big for me to pick up. Cole, who is six, will also be nine some day. And ten. And 18. And moving out and on with his life. I guess my point is to remind myself he's only little for a little while. What's 39 pounds when it's all made up of something you love beyond reason? Exactly. **AUGUST 2005**

scrapbooker, meet photo album

Photo album…meet scrapbooker. Now, go make nice, okay?

Photo albums are perhaps the single best solution for any scrapbooker with piles of photos. How can you feel guilty about those piles when your new best friend is as near as the photo aisle at your friendly neighborhood Target?

Photo albums serve an important purpose, even in a scrapbooker's life. What is that purpose? You put photos in them. This sounds too good to be true, but it isn't. Are you really planning to scrap every photo you take? How fun would that be? Pile after pile, mocking your lack of progress, making you buy scrapbook after scrapbook, and forcing your husband to build an addition to the house, to make room for more albums.

Simplify your scrapbook life. Scrap the photos and the stories that mean the most to you. It's not about quantity. No one will be handing out a "most photos scrapped" award at the pearly gates, if you get my drift.

Take for example the pics you see here, safely and appropriately tucked into the pages of my Kolo photo album. During construction on my block, the Lake Superior of mud puddles was formed. My kids and Aidan's best friend just couldn't resist. Me? I shot like a fiend, just as any good scrapbooking mom would do. When I was proofing the shots, I kept thinking of all

the pages I could make with these photos: *Getting Down n' Dirty*, or *Have Mud, Will Spatter*. But I don't really do pages like that. I don't scrapbook for the sake of scrapbooking. I feel no obligation to make a layout about my kids playing in a giant mud puddle. These photos are perfectly okay going into an album, with a few random notes in the margin.

However, I absolutely loved the photo of my daughter Aidan and her best friend, Nicolette, on the layout to the right. I made a quick page to highlight the shot.

The bottom line is this: live your life and enjoy it. Make scrapbooking a benefit and not an obligation. Use more photo albums for all those piles. Start today.

FRIEND

AND SOME MUCK TOO!

Aidan & Nicollette, 2005

THROUGH THICK AND THIN

GLORIFIED PHOTO ALBUMS

For some people, scrapbooking is a way to add pizzazz to what would otherwise be an ordinary photo album. Some people don't want to journal endlessly, or come up with clever ways to display and embellish their photos. They want to highlight their photos simply. End of story. And I love those people.

Narrow definitions just can't apply to this hobby. There are more ways to document the bits and pieces of your life than you can imagine. That's the truth. Even if you were only to create photo albums and write notes in the margins…guess what? I believe that is scrapbooking. Think about it: if scrapbooking combines photos and words to tell a story, then all expressions of this very fundamental definition apply. Scrapbooking is not exclusive. You don't need a special club membership card to get in. And you don't need to scrapbook all of your photos, either.

who are you, anyway?

A good question, don't you think? I only ask because how could I possibly know—or how could anyone else possibly know—if you don't include yourself as a regular scrapworthy subject. And why would I put this into a chapter about scrapbooking philosophy, as opposed to the chapter on journaling? Because if you read only one chapter in this book, it should be this one, and specifically, the next handful of paragraphs. I want to change the way you think about the content of your scrapbooking and how *you* fit into that picture.

Now, if you make pages about yourself on a regular basis, go to the mirror right now and say,

"Good scrapbooker." If you don't, read the following paragraph aloud, and with great feeling:

I am an interesting person, with unique perspectives and experiences. There isn't one person in this entire universe who lives a life like mine. I will choose to scrapbook about myself because I am a person of great value, and my stories should be told. Even if they are stories about how much I loathe doing laundry, wiping runny noses, working from nine to five, or any other random, mundane element that makes up my daily existence. My stories are important. And when I finish reading this section, I will put this book down, and make a simple page about myself.

ROLEPLAY

the wife

This is one I think, for the most part, I'm pretty good at. Dan is probably the reason why. He makes it easy, pretty much every day. Being a wife has helped me to become more selfless. Being a wife for five years before becoming a mother was a pretty good call. Being a wife also makes me feel loved. Who could really complain about that?

the mother

I'm okay at this one. I think sometimes I'm better than others. As a mother, I can play the "fun" role, and be silly and goofy. I think the one thing I have going for me is that I'm honest about life, my beliefs, and any other things that I think will help to expand the minds of my kids as they grow and help them turn into compassionate, caring humans. That part of the role I take very seriously.

the friend

I like being a friend, because being a friend has helped me to learn how to listen better, and be just a little less focused on all of my own drama. My circle of friends isn't huge, and I think I'm a far better long distance friend, but I try to be the right friend at the right time. As a friend, I can be completely myself...all the goofiness, neurosis, etc. And they still seem to like me. This is good.

the artist

For someone who makes her career in the creative arts, I don't really think of myself as an artist, however, I can't deny that the process of creating, whether it's scrapbook pages or layouts in magazines, is an artistic process. This is the role I relish. The role I've been protecting since I was nine years old. This is the role that allows me to express the stuff that's in my head, and in my heart.

Me

Cathy Zielske, 39
July 27, 2005

right now

Inside, I feel like I'm: 53.

A goal I'm working on right now: to not get stressed out over work.

My most recent achievement: three loads of laundry, folded and put away. The put away part is the victory.

The last gift I bought for someone: a doll from Creative Kidstuff for Erin's 3rd birthday.

The last CD I bought: The "Rise and Fall of Ziggy Stardust and the Spiders from Mars" by David Bowie, as a gift for Lin, because we agreed she needed some old Bowie.

My current favorite song: "Such Great Heights," by Iron & Wine. Such a lovely song.

The last movie I saw in a theater: Charlie and the Chocolate Factory.

The last book I read: "The Culture Clash," by Jean Donaldson.

The last new thing I learned: How to play the opening notes to Beethoven's "Moonlight Sonata," which I immediately forgot.

What I'm wearing right now: my orange sweatshirt (surprise!) and ripped up cargo pants.

The last person I talked to on the phone: Jeff Ess, who told me to get an agent.

What I ate for breakfast: half of a really bad egg and sausage sandwich from SA.

What I thought I'd be doing at this age: I never really imagined life beyond 30. I suppose I could say living in some cool loft with all white furniture.

Something I'm saving up for right now: a Digital Rebel. I'm so through with my Nikon.

Someone I think about alot: I hate to say it, but me. Man, that sounds pretty bad, huh?

The last person I helped: Cole, in the bathroom.

The last thing I apologized for: for being crabby to Aidan. I seem to do that with alarming frequency.

Something I'm worried about: me, or someone I love dying before their time.

What I wish for when I see a shooting star: the health and happiness of my family.

What my plans are for the rest of this day: worry some more about work but not actually work any more. Watch some bad television, pick up Dan and the kids from the Saints game, check my e-mail, and go to bed.

HAVE QUESTIONS, WILL ANSWER

This page was inspired by an article from *Simple Scrapbooks* magazine. Lists of questions were provided to help scrapbookers make pages about themselves by filling in the blanks. Simple. Telling. Done. If my daughter reads this when she's grown, I doubt she'll be thinking, "Mom, you were so vain!" I'd like to think she'll remember that we saw *Charlie and the Chocolate Factory* together. And that I was human. And that I valued myself enough to take the time to write down some words and take a picture. And that women celebrating themselves is a cool thing.

Thinking and talking about yourself feels weird, right? Perhaps because it rings a bit selfish? Narcissistic? Silly? Not really necessary in the overall scheme of scrap life? Not so!

MEMORY IS FLEETING

My mom, Shirley, is the most amazing mother on the planet. She is a model of patience and understanding. She never raised her voice to me or my brother. She would listen, she would advise, and even though we didn't always heed her advice, I think we knew we had a pretty good deal with her as our mom.

When I started scrapbooking, I wanted to know more about her life. What was it like to be a stay-at-home-mom in 1974? What was it like to manage a modest budget, and run a home, and care for two kids and assorted pets, and do everything else that came with the motherhood package?

When I ask her this, she says: "It was great. You kids were great."

But I know that she is lying.

I was the most high-strung kid ever to walk the earth circa 1974. I didn't sleep through the night until I was 9. I was a walking drama queen. There must have been days when Shirl was ready to pull her hair out, strand by blonde strand. There must have been times when my painstakingly picky eating habits made her want to send me to China to live with those starving children she so frequently told me about. There must have

been times when she wanted to be somewhere—anywhere—but right there in the thick and thin of domestic life. Right?

It's possible that my mom doesn't remember that I drove her nuts. Or that some days just keeping up with the laundry seemed like an impossible dream. But those are the things about her life that I really want to know. They probably didn't seem important or worth noting at the time. But they are, now, to me. I could connect with that, and find hope in it, and feel a different connection to her because of it.

The bottom line: take the time to record life. Your life. Not just the kids. Not just the holidays. Not just the big, giant exclamation marks that are so obviously scrapbook-worthy subjects. Scrapbook you.

It took two weeks

and just over 4,000 miles to get something I was sorely in need of—perspective. The three months leading up to our summer road trip to Seattle were a blur. I was finishing a book, working on far too many freelance jobs, trying to write articles, trying to keep up with my scrapbooking, flying to Utah, flying to Boston, and all the while trying to be a good wife and mother. And I was failing on the latter.

But two weeks away from my computer, and the phone, and everything work or scrapbook-related was exactly what I needed to remember that work is important, but that its place on the life pole needed to be bumped down a few notches. People needed clean clothes and hot food on the table. And most importantly, they needed me.

I think Dan and I both have the tendency to get so wrapped up in our deadlines, and the perceived importance of what we are doing for a living. But I'm not going to trade an hour with Cole to the television, just because I think I can check one more thing off my to-do list.

I didn't quit my job five years ago to see how many hours I could devote to my work. And the past three months of summer is time I can't get back. I can't undo my level of distraction and non-involvement.

But what I can do is keep the perspective. Work is fine, but family is foremost. That's officially the new mantra.

September 2004

life

p erspective

WHAT MAKES YOU TICK?

Here is a list, and by no means an exhaustive one, to get you thinking of ways you could get a little more of you into your scrapbooks. One thing to note: your children shouldn't be the primary focus of your answers. I know, kids are great, but this should be all about you.

- What makes you happy?

- If you could spend 24 hours walking in another person's shoes, whose would they be and why?

- Five random facts about you—the more random, the better! (see p. 35)

- What are your passions?

- What are some areas in your life you could improve?

- What do you do in the course of an average day? (complete with photos to illustrate!)

- What or who inspires you?

HAPPINESS CARD CERTIFIED
10 things that make me happy
1. MY NUTTY FAMILY
2. TIME ALONE
3. FLA·VOR·ICE
4. FRENCH FRIES
5. A CLEAN HOUSE
6. HUGS FROM AIDAN & COLE
7. ARGUMENT-FREE ZONES
8. SCRAPBOOKING
9. COMPUTER STUFF
10. CLEAN CLOTHES

HAPPINESS

Don't get me wrong, your kids will think the pages about their birthdays and holidays are great. But what they learn about you—who you are and were, what was in your heart and mind—is something they will connect to and identify with. It's something that will guide and inspire them in their adult lives. And it will sustain and support them when you are no longer gracing this earth with your physical presence. It will also help you to know more about the woman (or man) that you are today.

CHA 2005

I get to work with fun people. I don't know any other way to say it. I have this hobby, that turned into this amazing job. I travel places and see people I know and really like. It's like what skating meets used to be to me when I was a teenager. You all get together every three to four months, and just have a great flippin' time. In my head, I know it's a job. In my heart, I know it's what I'm supposed to be doing. I am lucky! This whole thing is **one ginormic, cool thing**. And yes, "ginormic" should be a word. It's so cool that Simple sends us to CHA. It is like the ultimate fix for any scrapbooker. A big old candy store. And you never even see a fraction of what is truly there. But it's always fun to stop by and say hi to the friends you make throughout the years and the shows. Yes, I loathe traveling and leaving my little nest, but once I get there, I have a great time. I connect with these people and remember what it is that we are all trying to do: **make a great magazine**. Everyone has ideas. Everyone has passion. THIS is the kind of job that inspires you to be the best that you can possibly be. This is the kind of job that, in the words of the keynote speaker Robyn Waters, makes you want to show **"grace and guts."** Yep. I work with really fun people. How cool is that?

BUT WHAT DO YOU THINK OF ME?

If you're uncomfortable scrapbooking about yourself directly, why not scrapbook about something that affects your life directly, like work. In this page above, even though it's about the people I work with, it's also indirectly a story about me. It's a start, right?

BUT THERE ARE NO PICTURES OF ME

Then hand the camera off to someone else once in a blue moon, would ya? Unless you have a self-timer, or freakishly long arms, you're going to have to ask for help. Force the issue, or there will be no visual record of yourself. I make my husband take a least one shot of me at any given event. Most of them are less than stellar, but they prove I was there and that I do, in fact, exist.

I AM SOMEWHAT OF AN OBSESSIVE-COMPULSIVE.

11.16.05

RANDOM *things*

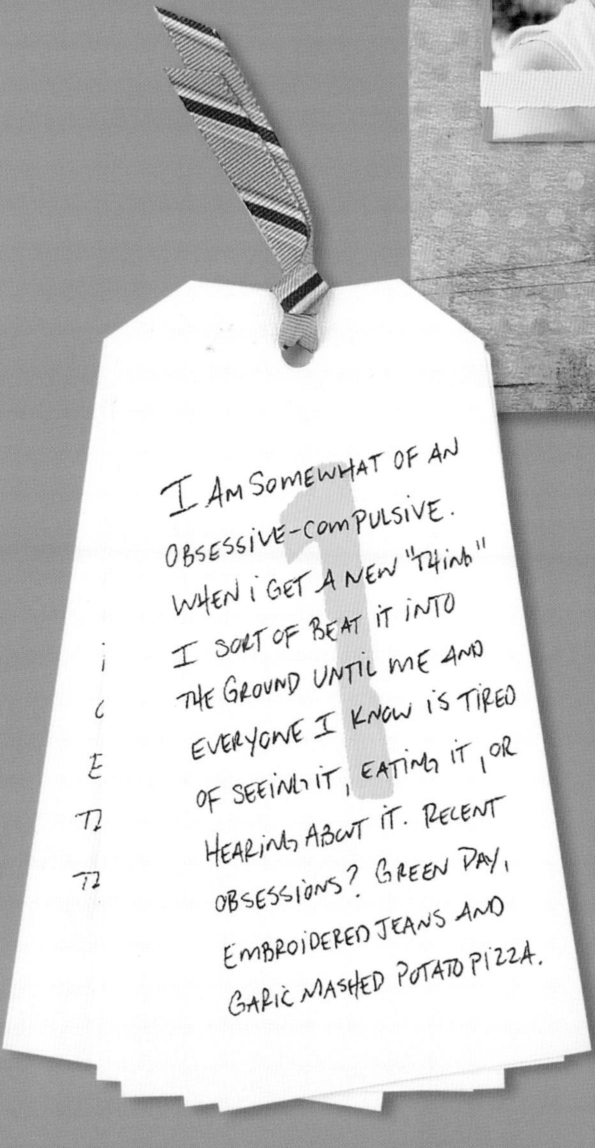

I AM SOMEWHAT OF AN OBSESSIVE-COMPULSIVE. WHEN i GET A NEW "THING" I SORT OF BEAT IT INTO THE GROUND UNTIL ME AND EVERYONE I KNOW IS TIRED OF SEEING IT, EATING IT, OR HEARING ABOUT IT. RECENT OBSESSIONS? GREEN DAY, EMBROIDERED JEANS AND GARLIC MASHED POTATO PIZZA.

ANYONE CAN DO THIS

This page was inspired by a game of blog tag, in which I was tagged by a fellow blogger to write five random facts about myself. It started a chain reaction in various online communities, and everyone was doing it. It's really easy and really fun. When you let yourself be a little more random in what you write about yourself, you realize it's no big deal. Anyone can do it.

Do it right now. It doesn't have to look anything like my page. Then, scan it and e-mail it to me. My contact info is in the back of this book. I won't post it on some underground web site. But I will thank you for it.

scrapbooking as therapy

Scrapbooking is good for your mental health. Aside from the joy of leaving a scrapbook store with a stash of new goodies to play with, the opportunity for scrapbooking to make us feel better is exponential. Whether it's creating a page that looks so dang good you want to do a victory dance, or simply capturing a slice of your life perfectly, the act of creating pages makes us feel like we are accomplishing something of value.

Part of what drew me to this hobby was the opportunity to explore, through words and images, all facets of life. Since I started my first diary at 11, I've worn down many a pencil tip musing about my life. From documenting how boy crazy I was at 15, to writing about the melodrama of being a teenager, to meeting and falling in love with my husband, I've kept a journal to record the highs and lows of my life.

For me, scrapbooking is really just visual journal keeping. I include observations, frustrations and other less-than-typical material on a regular basis when I scrapbook. If something's going on in my life that needs exploring, then it will surely end up in a scrapbook.

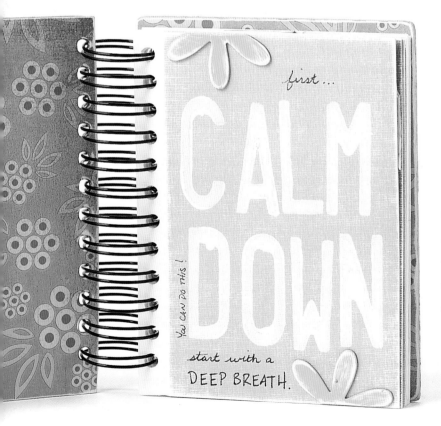

A LITTLE BOOK OF MANTRAS

This little album was a labor of self-help and love. I don't hide the fact that I live my life in extremes. It's part of what makes me "me." However, I decided to create a small album of mantras—personal reminders to myself—to help me calm down, live in the present, be thankful and strive to be a better person.

This album contains only one photo. It's more of a journal than anything. And it's written in the second person voice, so that when I pick it up for a pick-me-up, I'm hearing what it has to offer, directly from…well, me.

THIS IS A MESSAGE TO YOU.

YOU NEED TO STOP. RIGHT NOW. YOU TOOK THE DEEP BREATH. OKAY. THAT'S A START. HERE'S THE DEAL: YOU NEED TO BECOME A CALMER PERSON. YOU NEED TO BECOME LESS OF A PERFECTIONIST. YOU NEED TO BE NICER, MORE COMPASSIONATE AND MORE FUN. YOU NEED A REALITY CHECK. YOU WILL MAKE THIS ALBUM AND FILL IT WITH MANTRAS TO HELP YOU ACHIEVE THESE GOALS. LIFE REALLY ISN'T REFLECTED IN A CLEAN HOUSE. YOU WILL NOW BEGIN THIS EXERCISE.

I'M NOT TALKING HIP + COOL.

YOU KNOW WHAT I MEAN!

cool

BE AS COOL

AS YOU CAN BE!

SAY YOU'RE SORRY.

FOR SOMEONE WHO OFTEN LIKES TO GET THE LAST WORD IN... MAYBE TRY A DIFFERENT WORD, LIKE "SORRY." YOU HAVE A TENDENCY TO MAKE QUALIFIED APOLOGIES. "I'M SORRY, BUT..." JUST DON'T. SAY YOU'RE SORRY, MEAN IT, AND LET IT GO. DON'T HARBOR IT, AND GROW IT. BECAUSE IT WILL COME OUT IN ANOTHER FORM AT ANOTHER TIME, WITH ABSOLUTELY NO VALID CONNECTION TO THE ACTUAL MOMENT. AND THAT'S NOT GOOD. AND THAT'S NOT FAIR. YOU GETTIN' IT? PRACTICE BEING SORRY. DON'T HOLD GRUDGES. "BE THE CHANGE YOU WANT TO SEE." START BY SAYING SORRY...

sorry...

okay...

QUICKLY. FULLY. AND WITHOUT QUALIFICATION.

THIS IS A TOUGH ONE...

YOU SUFFER FROM VERBAL KNEE-JERK REACTIONS. AND YOU NEED TO CONTINUE TO WATCH HOW YOU USE AND CHOOSE WORDS. I KNOW, I REALLY REALLY KNOW HOW HARD IT CAN BE TO CONTROL AN IMPULSE. BUT YOU'VE GOT TO TRY TO GIVE ANY POTENTIALLY COMBUSTIVE WORDS AND PHRASES JUST A FEW EXTRA MICRO SECONDS TO BREW, BEFORE YOU LET THEM FLY. REMEMBER HOW IT FEELS TO BE ON THE RECEIVING END. USE YOUR WORDS TO IMPART LOVE, CONCERN, PRIDE, HAPPINESS AND EVEN CONFUSION. REMEMBER, THINK BEFORE YOU SPEAK!

ALWAYS STRIVE TO

think!

I KNOW IT'S HARD!

SPEAK. YELL. DISCIPLINE. GOSSIP. SWEAR. CORRECT. COMPLAIN. ARGUE. DEMAND.

Be thoughtful with words!

COUNT THE BLESSINGS.

BE CALM. BE SILENT, AND THANK GOD FOR EVERYTHING IN THIS LIFE. STOP. LOOK UP AT COLE WHILE HE'S RUNNING AROUND LIKE A BANSHEE. STOP. HUG AIDAN FOR ABSOLUTELY NO REASON. STOP. TELL DAN HOW MUCH YOU ADORE HIM. STOP AND JUST BE THANKFUL. REMEMBER WHAT MATTERS MOST. REMEMBER HOW BLESSED AND LUCKY YOU ARE. SHOUT IF FROM YOUR VERY SOUL. THANK YOU!

THE GIFTS...
TO BE THANKFUL.
TO BE HONEST.
TO BE KIND.
TO BE CREATIVE.
TO BE THOUGHTFUL.
TO BE SIMPLE!
TO WORK HARD BUT NOT TOO HARD. TO STAY FOCUSED on the stuff that TRULY MATTERS

don't forget!

BUT HEY— AT LEAST THIS PAGE HAS A PRETTY PICTURE!

AS A SCRAPBOOKER AND A PHOTOGRAPHER.....

STUCK

WHAT EXACTLY DO I MEAN BY "STUCK"?

STUCK...THAT IS HOW I FEEL RIGHT NOW IN MY CREATIVE HOBBY LIFE. STUCK AS A SCRAPBOOKER & STUCK AS A PHOTOGRAPHER. MY WORK LIFE IS JUST PEACHY... NO MISDIRECTION THERE. BUT HERE'S THE DEAL: I DECIDED TO GET MY PHOTOS INTO ALBUMS— TO BE CURRENT & CHRONOLOGICAL. AND ITS BASIC- ALLY KEPT ME FROM SCRAPBOOKING. THAT'S POINT A. POINT B: I DON'T EVEN KNOW, TRULY, WHAT I WANT TO SCRAPBOOK ABOUT. I DO NOT WANT TO SCRAP JUST FOR THE SAKE OF IT. I WANT SOME MEANING. ITS ALMOST LIKE I'M TAKING THE SIMPLE PHIL- OSOPHY TOO FAR. LATELY I'VE GOTTEN INTO MAKING THEME ALBUMS, BUT WHAT STARTS OUT WITH A BANG SEEMS TO FILL OUT W/ NOTHING. ITS LIKE I'VE GOT SCRAPBOOK ADHD. I CREATED A TITLE PAGE FOR AN ALL ABOUT ME ALBUM WITH THE LOVELY, MASSIVELY RETOUCHED PHOTO BELOW, AND THEN THOUGHT: WHY? WHAT IS TRULY THE POINT TO MAKING IT? I WANT TO HAVE FUN, AND CREATE AND DOCUMENT. I'M REALLY NOT ACCOMPLISHING ANY OF THAT RIGHT NOW. I THOUGHT I WOULD MAKE THIS PAGE TO TRY AND KICK START MY PROCESS. I'M NOT SURE IF ITS GOING TO WORK, BUT IT DID GIVE ME ROOM TO RAMBLE. HERE'S TO NOT RAMBLING ANYMORE AND GETTING BACK ON TRACK. 1.17.2005

BUT I'M NOT THE TOUCHY-FEELY TYPE

Scrapbooking is therapeutic. It doesn't have to be deep and confessional. I made the layout above after a long, dry spell of not scrapbooking. It was therapeutic because I used my own handwriting and some paint, and basically scrapped without thinking too hard about it.

The act of creating something from nothing is also therapeutic. You start with an idea, and grow it into something more. Something real. Something 100 percent, uniquely you. Remember, you don't have to write or photograph stuff that makes people cry. But hey, if you do? Bonus!

finding neverland

When people begin to scrapbook, the weirdest thing happens, and I've been trying to figure out how I missed out. It seems there is an underground travel agency that preys on new scrapbookers. They sell them advance tickets to a place called Caught Up.

Geographically speaking, I have no idea where Caught Up is, but here's what I've managed to piece together. Most scrapbookers who buy their tickets never actually take the trip. And the few who do manage to board that plane to this imaginary land of milk and Hermafix discover the following: a sterile hotel with rooms of completed albums carefully lined up on numerous shelves—and that's it. There are no organized activities. There are no excursions. There are no overflowing boxes of photos. There aren't even any scrapbooking supplies. There are only completed albums—nice ones, mind you—but that's it. It's very quiet there. And from what I hear, insanely boring. Same food. Same scenery. Same finished albums. And the scrapbookers are scratching their heads, wondering, "So this is the place I was trying so hard to get to?"

It reminds me of a quote from one of my childrens' favorite movies, *Austin Powers 2: The Spy Who Shagged Me*: "Whoop de do, what does it all mean, Basil?"

What it means to me is this: when scrapbooking is a means to an end, instead of a process, it's just not going to be as fun as it could be. When you decide you are behind from the get-go, you are actually buying yourself a one-way ticket to Stressville. And don't you have enough stress in your life as it is?

Scrapbooking is a process; a fluid, creative, memory-laden journey. It lets you feel alive and in touch with the richness of life. It lets you document the experience of being human. It's so much bigger than finished albums on a shelf in perfect, chronological order.

So if you've already bought that ticket, return it. Be a person who never stops exploring the process. Finish pages and be proud of what you've created. Don't lose joy to the notion that you should be somewhere called Caught Up, and that lots of other people are there, having the time of their lives.

Remember these two words—insanely boring.

Or at least that's what I've heard.

buck

A buck. One greenback. A single dollar. That is what it cost me to take the above photograph. Aidan has officially put a price tag on being photogenic. The problem is this: I want to get better at using my digital camera. I want to know that I can get images as good as I can with film. In order to get better, one needs to practice. I only have two subjects, really. (Dan is cute, don't get me wrong, but...) And so, I have Aidan and Cole. Cole flat out loathes sitting still for two minutes, and always gives me the cheesiest, over-wrought grin he can muster. So this leaves Aidan, who truly can turn it on for the camera. But, she's sick of it at this point. That's where the money comes into play. She's no fool to know that every dollar earned is one step closer to a trip to Toys R Us. And so, I bribe. After getting my new reflector set from Dan for Christmas, I really wanted to play, to see how reflecting and diffusing can affect a shot. So I pried Aidan away from the Neo Pets online game she was playing with a phrase that I'm afraid will get a lot more common in the months to come: "Hey kid, wanna make a buck?"

JANUARY 2005

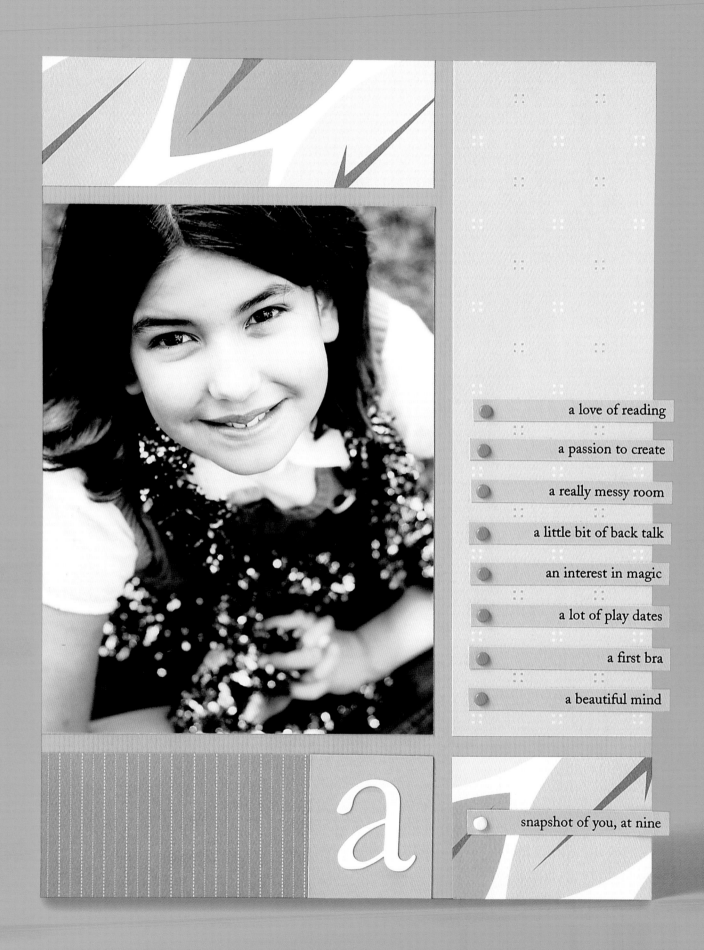

a love of reading

a passion to create

a really messy room

a little bit of back talk

an interest in magic

a lot of play dates

a first bra

a beautiful mind

a

snapshot of you, at nine

share

Once upon a time, there was a girl who liked to write down

stories. She wasn't very good at making up stories, but

she was good at reporting the ones from her own life.

Then she started scrapbooking. Now she wants to help other

scrapbookers learn to share their stories, too. She also

wants world peace and to meet the lead singer of the

Foo Fighters. But then again, don't we all?

dear diary, today I...

I've decided to keep a second diary because it is something you can tell anything to. I really do hope that my New Year's resolution (wish) comes true. Are you ready for this one? To go out with Jim Garberich!!!! That's all I want. I don't know why I like him so much cuz I don't know him that well. Oh well! My brother is 18 today. I hope this year turns out to be the best of all. And, I'll try to make what I write more exciting, O.K? But, it's not my fault if it's boring.

— taken from 15-year-old Cathy (Zielske) MacDonald's 1981 diary, unedited (as today, I would never use four exclamation marks in a row).

I've always liked writing. Even when I was 15 and all my writing involved boys and excessive punctuation.

I kept it up over the years. Diary after diary, and journal after journal. And while most of of those diaries and journals are heavily dosed with teen angst, they are time capsules of what went on in my heart and mind as I grew into the semi-well-adjusted adult I am today.

Scrapbooking is really no different. It offers a singular opportunity to write about your life in a way that is personal and uniquely you.

I can't promise to make you a better writer, but I can offer ideas and examples of how I share the stories of my own life. I can hope that you relate to kids who don't listen, sinks overflowing with dirty dishes, friends who make you smile and moments almost too magical for words. That's my goal, anyway.

Are you ready to write?

wake up
brush teeth
take a shower
wear the same jeans
check my e-mail
make coffee
read the paper

get kids up
feed kids cinnamon toast
throw in a load of laundry
empty the dishwasher
pack lunches
yell if they're arguing
kiss them at the bus stop

EVERY·DAY

start working
play music loudly
check more e-mail
post on my blog
work more
eat the same lunch
talk on the phone

watch 10 minutes of Oprah
before kids get home
give snacks and hugs
yell more if they are arguing
attempt to make some
form of dinner
check e-mail
fold laundry

laugh at something
create something
day dream about something
read about something
accomplish something
and above all,
be thankful for **everything**

LOOK MA, JUST WORDS!

Everybody does stuff every day. If you write down a handful of those things and use them on a scrapbook page, you've got one small dose of authentic journaling about your life. Easy and painless. I did this on the layout above. It's a list of the things I do on any given day. (Except I wish I could get more than 10 minutes of Oprah. Note to self: do layout on why I need TiVo.)

say what you mean, part one

We had fun!

This phrase should be banned from the English language. It says nothing. It means nothing. One big pile of verbal nothingness.

Many women feel they aren't natural writers. "It's easy for you," they tell me. "You're a good writer!" I'm only a good writer because I have practiced saying what I mean, over and over again. Saying what you mean doesn't necessarily come naturally. For some crazy reason, you might be the most adept conversationalist in the world, but when it comes to writing what you mean, you turn into robo-writer: stiff, dull and predictable.

But I'd wager a bet on this: you're not a robot in real life, right? You talk, and laugh, and yell, and rant and rave. (Okay, I rant and rave; you, maybe not quite as much.) The point is, if you listen to how you talk in real life, you can begin to apply the style to your writing. You can learn to say what you mean. I mean it!

thankful for you

For better or worse... we said those words, and while I have no doubt that we meant them, I think at the time they were spoken, they were just that—words. One vital event must take place before the meaning of those words really comes into focus: the passing of time. And more specifically: years. That's when the definition crystalizes. That's when you begin to understand.

Everyone likes 'better'. 'Better' is fun. 'Better' is easy. 'Better' lets you sleep at night. 'Worse' is what separates the men from the boys. 'Worse' defines your character. 'Worse' hands you the singular chance to grow.

I wanted you to know that my love for you isn't in spite of better or worse. It's because of it. There will always be bumps. Always. It's the long haul. I'm here for it. So are you. It's something that shines, even if you have to dust a few things away from time to time in order to see the shimmer. I love you, Dan, for better and worse.

PARDON MY EXPRESSION

I love to use common expressions as a starting place for my journaling. The words "for better or for worse" are pretty standard for anyone who's ever taken the leap into marriage.

I'd been thinking a lot about this in the fall of 2004. My husband, Dan, has suffered from depression periodically throughout his life. For many years, I simply didn't understand it. Why didn't he just pull himself up by the bootstraps and get over it? Why not choose to be happy?

Then I had my second child and went through a bout of postpartum depression. It was the best thing that could've happened to me, in a way, because it let me understand part of the man with whom I share my life. It also reminded me how committed I am to our union. For better, or for worse.

thankful
for 16 years with you

For the little things. For the big things. For the rare night out when we get to talk in complete sentences. For your endless reserve of patience. For your perfectly timed Hannibal Lecter impersonations. For your attraction to me. For your mother, simply for having you. For your parents, who raised a boy into a sensitive, thoughtful and responsible man. For your parenting skills. For your practical nature. For your calming effect. For 16 years together. For meeting you at the right time and the right place. For staying up all night and watching the Jerry Lewis Telethon. For the moment when our knees touched. For the fact that you get me, and still seem to like me. For being lucky enough to share the whole kit and kaboodle with you.

SAY IT, THEN REPEAT IT

Verbal repetition is one of the easiest ways to construct a solid block of journaling. You simply repeat a key word or phrase, over and over, and fill in the details.

You can do this. Pick a subject—like gratitude—and list what you are thankful for, like I did. I'm thankful for...and fill in the blank. It works really well when your subject is a person. People inspire the strongest memories and feelings. Capitalize on that. Make a page about someone you're thankful for. Use verbal repetition, and see just how good you are at saying what you mean.

telling simple stories

Once upon a time, a scrapbooker made a nice, simple page and told a good story. The end.

We'll get to how to make a nice-looking, simple page in Chapter 3. Now, let's talk about how to write a good story. First, define what makes a good story, as opposed to a boring one. Here's the secret: there really are no boring stories. There are only choices you make in how to share them. I'm no writing instructor, but I've got a few ideas to help you kick up your writing a notch or two.

JUMP IN THE WATER

I also love to write layout titles. I'm not sure why, but most of the time my mind works like a small ad agency, generating punchy, succinct, and slightly quirky titles. And if I really like the title, I'll repeat it in the journaling.

This can also work in reverse. When you finish writing your journaling, read it back and see if something you wrote can be pulled out and used as a title. It makes a nice link for anyone reading your page.

TRY WRITING LIKE THIS

1. Write in a second person voice. You did [blank]. You were [blank]. Using "you" is immediately more personal and engaging than third person (he/she did [blank]).

2. Ask questions while you write. On my "Kindergarten" page at right, I asked the question: would you be exhausted by 2 p.m.? When you pose questions in your writing, you get to answer them, giving you more ways to tell your story.

BIG
swimmin' DEAL

HOW COLE MADE IT THROUGH PIKE WITH MINIMAL FEAR

You did it. You completed a session of swimming lessons with hardly a single panic attack. You think I'm exaggerating? Even though you have no problems going into the lake up at the cabin, when it comes to a pool with chlorine and instructors, you've had the tendency in the past to, well, freak out. But this spring, you managed to keep your head above water, and keep your cool in swimming class. Sure, you'll probably repeat Pike three to six times in the next two years, but hey, this is definitely a major, major accomplishment in your young life. Great job, buddy. It's a big swimmin' deal. **May 2005**

September 2005—light years away from September 2004, when you stepped on a school bus for the very first time. This year, it was Kindergarten. Old school, really. You were heading back to the same room with Ms. Kaniainen. No sweat. Not a drop. You had the same backpack, and it still dwarfed you, but not nearly as much as last year. Inside, your Darth Vader lunch box was filled with the standard fare: peanut butter and jelly, chips, Oreos, a Slim Jim and a frozen Go-Gurt. The only thing I worried about was the transition from half-day friend to all-day friend. Not that you're a nap-takin' kind of kid, but I worried: would you be exhausted by 2 p.m.? But all that would come to pass in time, as you adjusted to the change. For this morning, it was simply a confident, happy, six-year-old boy heading off for his first day of kindergarten. With no tears in sight.

kindergarten

first day

LAME TITLE, BUT GOOD STORY

I realize my title on this page isn't all that catchy. For the life of me, I have the hardest time spacing rub-ons correctly. It took me forever to finally get the word "kindergarten" lined up. So, I guess that's why I cut myself some slack on the lame title. I'm trying more and more to let go of my perfectionist tendencies. I need to remember that for me, the story is the most important thing. If I can get that down, the rest can slide from time to time.

1. Assume a character voice other than your own. Sound goofy? When I read the "Taco Night" layout below, I imagine myself as a boxing ring announcer. *Ladies and Gentlemen... tonight, one family eats the same thing.* I know it seems silly, but when you're making a silly layout, why not?

2. When journaling about a given topic, reference other memories from different times and places. No one lives in a vacuum. Almost everything we experience in life can be tied to a previous experience. When you're scrapbooking a story, stop for a moment and ask yourself if this triggers any other past memories. If so, go ahead and add, "It reminds me of the time I, you, we..."

SIMPLE AS...TACOS?

I don't expect to get any design awards for this layout, but it makes me smile. When I realized that, for once, every member of my small family would eat the same meal, it was big news. News worthy of scrapbooking.

The task was simple: create a report, complete with facts, figures and photos, about Australia. In fine Zielske fashion, Aidan sort of, well, **procrastinated** is a bit strong, but in essence, we realized at 6 p.m. one evening that it was due the following day. Enter a panicked mother, some random notes on Australia from said child, and a G5 Mac with all the trimmings. We would not only succeed in creating the most rocking of all reports on Australia, but we would also succeed in leaving all other third graders in our wake. It reminded me of a *Saturday Night Live* commercial from some time during the '90s. It was a parody of a Macintosh commercial with the tagline, **"The Power to be Your Best."** It showed these little kids working on their school reports. Some kids were using crayons, glue and other typical school supplies. One kid had a Mac at home. His report was complete with color photos, charts, diagrams—you name it. The SNL tagline at the end? **Macintosh: The Power to Crush Other Kids**. It made me laugh then. It makes me laugh now. I realized my goal was to help Aidan master the Mac and create a report that would crush other children. Does that make me a bad person? Sorry, but if there's one thing my kid's going to learn, along with how to be a decent human being and how to clean her room, it's how to design a report board with great typesetting and no trapped white space. That's just non-negotiable.

Or, the story of how Aidan used Apple technology and a little help from Mom to annihilate all third grade pretenders to the throne

MAY 2005

CROSS REFERENCE MEMORIES

Do you ever mix your memories? I do it all the time. One memory is part of the making of another memory. In this layout, a memory of an old *Saturday Night Live* parody commercial melded into the making of the actual memory I was scrapbooking. I think that sometimes, when we leave journaling to the end, it's a hasty rush to throw something down and be done with it. For me, it's always the reverse. Make sure there's a story first, then throw down a photo. One of the main reasons I scrap so many single photo pages is I really want room to record the memory in words.

DISASTER

Okay, technically, his middle name is "Asher," but with his latest five-year-old obsessions, we may as well file the paper work and have it officially changed. It all started with the Titanic. Somehow, he managed to get me to let him watch that big budget, Leo DiCaprio tour-de-force (fast forwarding through the topless Kate Winslet part and the floating dead bodies, of course) and since that time, there's been no turning back. Every week on library night, he would return with assorted books and videos covering the legendary disaster. Then, he soaked up the facts and figures like a sponge.

Ask him anything…go on, we dare you! Name of the lookout on duty that night? Frederick Fleet. Time the great ship struck the berg? 11:40 p.m. Time it actually succumbed to the icy waters of the North Atlantic? 2:20 a.m. Name of the legendary band leader who played until the ship sank? Wallace Hartley. Were there enough lifeboats for all of the 2,200 passengers? Not even by half. The man who discovered the Titanic in 1985? Robert Ballard? Name of the sub he used to go down and explore? Alvin. He recites this stuff to anyone who will listen. He's a walking Titanic almanac.

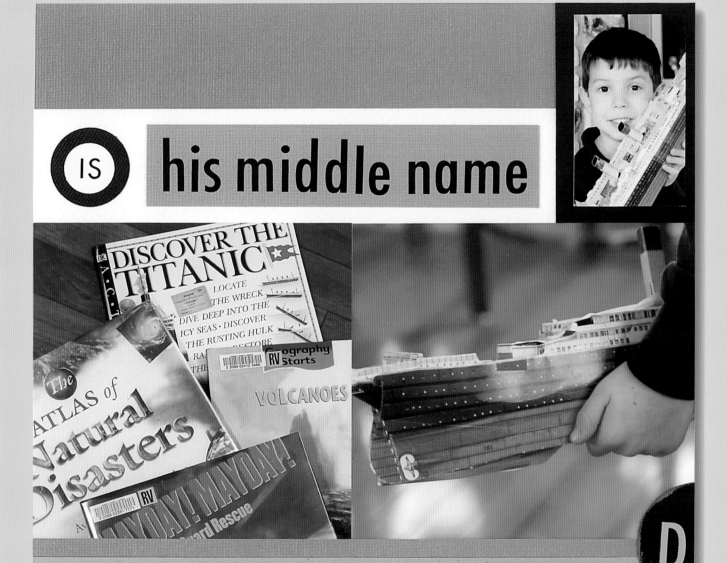

IS his middle name

But as if obsessing about one disaster wasn't enough, he found a new object of interest: natural disasters. Floods, hurricanes, earthquakes, tornados, tsunamis, mud slides and volcanic eruptions, just to name a few. And so began a new library cycle: books and videos covering all of them. Story time at our house has turned into part science class and part horror story, really. He recently brought home a "Where's Waldo" book and asked me to read it at bedtime. My jaw just about dropped to the floor. "Huh? No devastating avalanche stories tonight?" Go figure.

And so he continues on his quest to learn as much about disasters as possible. He even checked out two books on the Hindenburg. I'm not too worried about this phase. I watch him play in the family room, re-enacting the Titanic sinking with his paper model of the ship and a cast of unsuspecting Lego guys, complete with all the sound effects of the scraping iceberg and screaming passengers, and I just smile. He's a kid with a thirst for knowledge and a ripe imagination. But not only that, he's got stone cold scientific facts to back it all up. NOVEMBER 2004

reflect your life

Kids are great, but there is so much more to scrapbook about. Our lives are so rich with raw material, it's ridiculous. Yes, even yours. You say, "But my life isn't really all that interesting." And I say, "Wrong!"

Everyone has something that makes them happy, excited, obsessed, perturbed, or even angry. We are complex creatures. There is so much stuff in my life that has absolutely nothing to do with being a mother and a wife, and it deserves to go into my scrapbooks. I am documenting the entire experience. Whether it's my obsession with heavily-tattooed rock singers, or the fact that I

love Flavorice more than any other sweet treat in the world. Or, that I really like my job and feel incredibly lucky that I work from home, and that if I wear the same clothes every day, no one knows. Or, that having central air conditioning installed in my house has been quite possibly the greatest creature comfort I have ever attained.

My point: dig a little deeper into what makes you tick, and scrapbook it. From the frivolous to the profound, there is more to you than meets the eye. Share it in your pages.

DAVE GROHL

BILLIE JOE

GREEN DAY AND FOO FIGHTERS ARE CURRENTLY ROCKING MY UNIVERSE.

Not pretty. Definitely not pretty. In the traditional sense anyway. A little messy. A little threadbare. Tattoos are always a plus. When they sing, they have to mean it. You know when they mean it. That's a requisite. Lead guitar is always a nice touch, but it's not required. If they're political, it doesn't hurt. Humor is good. If they are witty and clever in their interviews, it only adds to their rock star caché. They need to make me wish, for a slight second, that I could've been a rock star, too. They need to make me have fun. It's not a lofty list when you think about it. I'm not leaving Peter Gabriel off this list per se. He's the godfather. A different class. He makes me cry. These guys? They just make me remember how much I love to rock it out. That, and let's face it—they're scorchingly HOT!

G5 lovin'

11.04—THE BEST MONTH EVER!

Speed

" YES... I'LL TAKE ONE STATE-OF-THE-ART MAC, PLEASE."
I HAVE LONGED TO SAY THOSE WORDS SINCE MY VERY
FIRST MAC PURCHASE, SOME COUNTLESS YEARS AGO.
BUT UP UNTIL NOW, IT WAS ALWAYS THE MID-RANGE
MACHINES. THE "BUY THIS BECAUSE YOU REALLY CAN'T
AFFORD THAT ONE" MACHINES. THE "MAKE YOU
YEARN FOR SO MUCH MORE" MACHINES. BUT THANKS
TO THE PROCEEDS FROM "CLEAN & SIMPLE," I NOW
HAVE MY FIRST-EVER TOP 'O THE LINE MAC. WANT
TO OPEN 20 PHOTOSHOP FILES AT ONCE? NO PROBLEMO.
LET'S FACE IT: i NEED THIS SPEED! NO MORE TIME
SPENT WATCHING THE SPINNING RAINBOW BALL.
IT'S OFFICIAL: i AM TOTALLY COOL AND A GEEK
AT THE SAME TIME. I LOVE YOU, LITTLE DUAL
2.5 GHZ G5. AND i AM NOT ASHAMED TO SAY SO!

WHAT DO YOU LOVE?

Forget about the people in your life for now. Focus on the stuff you love. Me? My computer. It makes me happy, it gives me a career, and it lets me reach out to people all over cyber space. In the fall of 2004, I bought the mother lode of all Macs—a dual 2.5 ghz G5. It was the first time I've ever owned a state-of-the-art-machine. Scrapworthy? As they say in Minnesota, you betcha!

{ 1 0 r e a s o n s w h y }

I ~~like~~ love! my job

Simple Scrapbooks™

Cathy Zielske
Creative Director

www.simplescrapbooksmag.com   **E-mail** czdesign@comcast.net

1. I absolutely love working as a graphic designer. No two days or jobs are exactly the same. Variety is king.

2. The subject matter is actually something I am passionate about.

3. I work from home sweet home, where you can take lunch when you feel like it and listen to Peter Gabriel all day long.

4. I can wear the same clothes every day and no one in the office has to know. No wardrobe budget needed.

5. The smell of freshly printed ink on paper makes me happy.

6. The people I work for are ultra-humane and really, really cool.

7. I love the problem solving that comes whenever you start a new project. How to make stuff go where it should, and look good in the process. It makes me feel smart.

8. My only office mate is my G5 and it never has a harsh word.

9. I get paid for what I'm doing.

10. I can't imagine anything else that would be as much fun.

We've been together for nearly two years…two years of laughter, happiness and much, much lower humidity. I don't know if I tell you enough how much I appreciate everything you've done for me. Reducing my heat-induced headaches. Making me not fear the dog days of summer. Running so quietly that two people can actually carry on a conversation. Sometimes, I just want to go outside and wrap my arms around you, but I'm afraid of what the neighbors will think. You're so adorable at 74 degrees, and downright irresistable at 73. Sometimes, when I'm totally caught up in the moment, I run you at 72. Then you're off the charts. (This, of course, is the only time Dan has a problem with our special relationship.) So thank you, Heil Max Performance 12 air cooling system. You make my life a happier, much less sticky place to be for roughly four months each year. I can't imagine how I lived for through so many sub-tropical Minnesota summers without you. Until next May, sweet prince…

central
kind of love

HAVE A LITTLE FUN

Scrapbooking about the details of your life need not be an exploration of your deepest self. Layouts about central air conditioning or Flavorice may not seem important in the grand scheme of things. And they won't solve a single world problem. But they will place a small, telling magnifying glass directly upon the story teller: you.

say what you mean, part two

Think of yourself as a reporter. Your beat is the Variety Section, covering the people, places and things that make up your life. You need to be observant, always on the lookout for the next big story. The better you get at being aware, the larger your pool of story material becomes.

To tell a story, you don't have to be a good writer. Really. If you can begin by recording the who, what, when and where, then you're off to a good start. The trick is jumping into the why of it all. That's where the true story lies. You need to uncover the "whys" of your stories. Then things begin to get interesting.

For example, my son has an imaginary friend named Francis. So I asked a few questions. Who is Francis, anyway? His replies gave me the "whys" to write the story and make the page. This is the key to every good story. Always ask "why?"

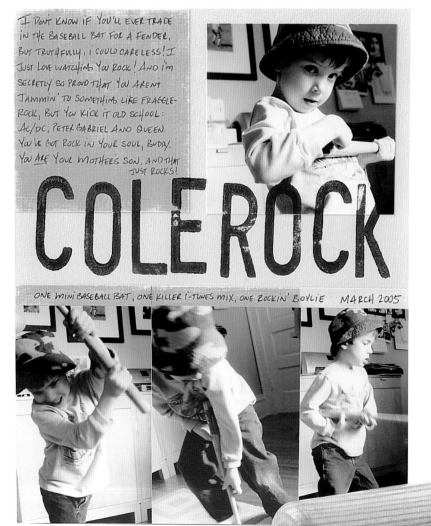

I DON'T KNOW IF YOU'LL EVER TRADE IN THE BASEBALL BAT FOR A FENDER, BUT TRUTHFULLY, I COULD CARE LESS! I JUST LOVE WATCHING YOU ROCK! AND I'M SECRETLY SO PROUD THAT YOU AREN'T JAMMIN' TO SOMETHING LIKE FRAGGLE-ROCK, BUT YOU KICK IT OLD SCHOOL: AC/DC, PETER GABRIEL AND QUEEN. YOU'VE GOT ROCK IN YOUR SOUL, BUDDY. YOU ARE YOUR MOTHER'S SON. AND THAT JUST ROCKS!

COLE ROCK

ONE MINI BASEBALL BAT, ONE KILLER I-TUNES MIX, ONE ROCKIN' BOYLIE   MARCH 2005

PHOTOS TELL THE STORY

Cole rocks. Literally. If some rocking tune comes on, he bolts for the baseball bat, and proceeds to get heavy with his metal. A lot of journaling isn't needed to get this across. Just a few words from me—his future band manager—about how cool it is that he likes to rock.

In addition to focusing on the "whys" of any given story, you also have to include the "yous," meaning your thoughts and feelings as they relate to the story you are telling. Injecting "I" into any journaling gets a little more of you and your viewpoints onto the page.

who is FRANCIS

So just who *is* Francis? A fine question, and well worthy of further exploration. Let us begin...

Francis is Cole's imaginary friend. He made his debut at some point during the past two years, and today is involved in pretty much everything Cole does. But what do we *really* know about Francis? Here's what we've assessed thus far, thanks to a little help from Cole:

1. Francis is from Boston.

2. Francis has black hair, wears glasses, and is, not surprisingly, the same age as Cole.

3. Francis has a twin brother named Lawrence, who also now lives at our house.

4. Francis also has a sister named Leia, who showed up rather conveniently after Cole watched the *Star Wars* video. I'm not certain if she too lives at our house, or just visits.

I never had an imaginary friend, myself, unless you count my imaginary horse, Pal, whom I played with as a kid. I love to listen in on Cole's wild imaginary play when Francis is involved. He helps Cole battle hurricanes and tornadoes, and even attempts to save the sinking Titanic with him, nearly every day. I think a part of me just envies the magic of what a child knows, that adults will never be able to see or truly remember. Hey Coley, tell Francis he is always welcome here. You'll miss him when he eventually goes away. [MARCH 05]

be specific—B-E-specific

I am a lucky person. I live in a world populated with the most passionate, charismatic, kind, interesting and crazy people you could ever hope to meet. And that's just my family.

But my circle has widened over the years, and there are so many people I now consider friends. When you stop to think about your friends, I'll bet it's easy to recall details about why you like these people. Am I right?

When journaling about the people who make up your world, be specific. This is not a time to speak in sweeping generalities. When it comes to writing about people, include the bits and pieces that answer the following questions:

1. Who are they? (to you? to their families?)

2. What do they do? (work? raise kids? make you laugh? restore your faith in friendship?)

3. What do they mean to you? (the go-to friend? the "I could use a laugh" friend? the one who always listens without judgment?)

Start with a friend in mind and a photo, and begin making random statements about that person. Be specific. They aren't just *nice*, so you have to write more than that. Like, they'd talk you off an emotional ledge, even if you needed it at 3 a.m. You see where I'm going, right? Tell it like it is.

she is a woman. she is a wife. she is a mother. she is an artist. she paints with light in ways that take many breaths away. she is wickedly funny, even though she may not realize it. she is calm on the surface, while things below might actually be swirling out of control. she is compassionate. she is unique. she is also deathly afraid of small rodents and birds, which I find highly amusing. she is a hippie in her soul. she has a guitar that I know in my heart she's going to learn to play. she's a california girl through and through. she is a really good person and people are lucky to know her. lucky me...because she is my friend.

SCRAPBOOK YOUR FRIENDS

At last count, I have six pages that celebrate my friend, Tara. Why? Because I like her—a lot. And because she is an integral part of my circle, even though she lives half-way across the country from me. I talk to her at least twice a week on the phone, e-mail her every day, and when I've been on those emotional ledges, she's talked me down.

That's friendship. It's big stuff. I pay tribute to her by scrapbooking about our friendship, and in turn, I remind myself how blessed I am to have such a good friend.

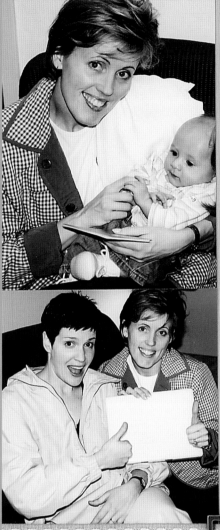

Do you know my friend, Stacy? You know, Stacy Julian, founder of *Simple Scrapbooks* magazine Stacy? Scrapbooking philosophy innovator Stacy? So-popular-you're-lucky-to-get-her-class-at-CKU Stacy? Yeah, I thought you did! Well, I think the best part about all the roles she fills in the scrapbooking and real world, aside from being a mother, wife and overall superstar, is that of being my friend. I will never forget the first time she called me. I had some friends over, and the phone rang, and I covered the receiver and yelled, "Mother of Pearl! It's Stacy Julian from *Simple Scrapbooks* magazine!" Of course, my guests gave me the 100-mile blank stare (not a scrapbooking group, mind you) and didn't quite share in my over-the-top excitement. That was nearly two years ago. Since then, so much has happened and my life course altered greatly. Who knew I'd get to work for such a cool magazine writing about things I love, like design and typography? Who would have ever thought I could get up in front a group of 80 women and keep them entertained *and* educated? Who would have ever thought anyone in their right mind would ask me to sign an autograph? Well, maybe Stacy thought so. Yeah, I think she had a vision. But the coolest thing about all of the events of the past few years is this: I have this friend, and her name is Stacy. And she has more integrity and passion in her little finger than you can shake a stick at. I feel honored to work for her, but moreso to be her friend. I once said if she asked me to jump off a building, I probably would! Here's to you, Stacy. Thanks for being my friend. And may tall buildings and jumping never become a new hot trend in scrapbooking!

my friend

stacy
10.15.03

report what you hear

When you don't know what to write, let the subjects do the talking. More and more, I include snippets of what people say when I'm telling a story on a layout. In fact, one of my biggest inspirations to create a page comes after someone has said something. Usually, it's my kids, because they are hilarious and brilliant, and I feel like everything that comes out of their mouths is scrapworthy. But that's just me.

This approach puts you back into reporter mode. You have to keep track of what people say. You have to jot it down on a scrap of paper, or put it into a small notebook.

You have to open your ears for the revelations, the insights, the amazing ideas or just the plain old silly stuff.

So much of what people say is a reflection of who they are. I decided to write down some of my husband's expressions, because he says them all the time, and they always make me laugh. This is the ultimate exercise in ultra-specific scrapbooking. It's not about the photos at all. It's about the people, and the wacky, sincere and even predictable things they say. And that makes for some good scrapbooking. Trust me. Heck, you can even quote me.

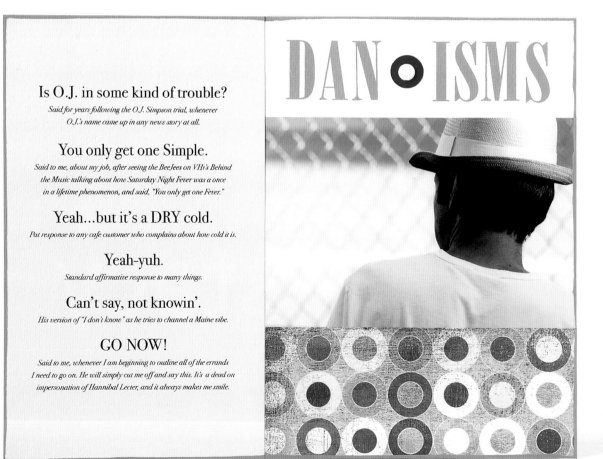

Is O.J. in some kind of trouble?
Said for years following the O.J. Simpson trial, whenever O.J.'s name came up in any news story at all.

You only get one Simple.
Said to me, about my job, after seeing the BeeJees on VH1's Behind the Music talking about how Saturday Night Fever was a once in a lifetime phenomenon, and said, "You only get one Fever."

Yeah...but it's a DRY cold.
Pat response to any cafe customer who complains about how cold it is.

Yeah-yuh.
Standard affirmative response to many things.

Can't say, not knowin'.
His version of "I don't know" as he tries to channel a Maine vibe.

GO NOW!
Said to me, whenever I am beginning to outline all of the errands I need to go on. He will simply cut me off and say this. It's a dead on impersonation of Hannibal Lecter, and it always makes me smile.

DAN•ISMS

ROCK SAND

WE ARE IN THE PARKING LOT AT ARCHIVER'S, AND COLEY SAYS, "MOM, KNOCK-KNOCK!" AND I SAY, "WHO'S THERE?" AND HE SAYS, WHILE HOLDING A ROCK IN HIS HAND, "ROCK." TO WHICH I REPLY, "ROCK WHO?" AND HE SAYS, "ROCK," WHILE SHOWING ME HIS ROCK, AND THEN, LOOKING DOWN AT THE GRAVEL AND SAND ON THE ROAD, HE SAYS, "SAND...GET IT? ROCK-SAND?" AND I JUST STARTED LAUGHING, AND HE SAID, "MOM, IT'S A JOKE ABOUT THE POLICE. GET IT?" ONE OF HIS FAVORITE SONGS OF LATE IS ROXANNE, BY STING & COMPANY. NOW IS THAT A CLEVER KNOCK-KNOCK JOKE, OR WHAT? I REST MY CASE! APRIL 2004

HOW COLEY TELLS A KNOCK-KNOCK JOKE AND PROVES ONCE AND FOR ALL, HE IS A COMPLETE AND TOTAL GENIUS.

KNOCK KNOCK. WHO'S THERE?

Cole's Police-inspired knock-knock joke killed me. I remember thinking: you are your mother's son. Any time a kid takes a classic rock and roll song and turns it into a knock-knock joke, it deserves a layout.

And I truly believe that if I hadn't written this down, I would not remember it today. This is the kind of thing that can potentially be lost for all time. Don't lose the verbal gems. Scrapbook them today.

you might miss it

If you blink. You've heard this, right? This is how I feel about storytelling and scrapbooking. If we blink, and just fill our scrapbooks with lots and lots of nice photographs and few words, we are missing the stories of a lifetime.

Are you one of those people who started this hobby long after your kids were out of diapers? And you're thinking about the monumental task of going back and gathering all those baby photos to document the story of your child's life?

Here's my advice to you: don't do it. You don't have to go back and start from square one. Start from where you are. Create a page that compares and contrasts your child today with what you recall from earlier years. I'm doing this more and more on pages about my daughter because I didn't scrapbook when she was little.

Do the best with what you have—which is the here and now. Don't lament what you can't recall, or didn't record. Just focus on the stories you can tell. Then, get writing.

imagination

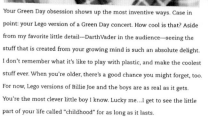

Your Green Day obsession shows up the most inventive ways. Case in point: your Lego version of a Green Day concert. How cool is that? Aside from my favorite little detail—DarthVader in the audience—seeing the stuff that is created from your growing mind is such an absolute delight. I don't remember what it's like to play with plastic, and make the coolest stuff ever. When you're older, there's a good chance you might forget, too. For now, Lego versions of Billie Joe and the boys are as real as it gets. You're the most clever little boy I know. Lucky me...I get to see the little part of your life called "childhood" for as long as it lasts.

Where is that sweet-cheeked, happy little baby girl that lived with us for such a short time? How is it that in a figurative blink, she became this new, sweet-cheeked happy medium-sized girl we see everyday? From almost one to almost nine...did we blink? I know we didn't miss a thing, but why is it that I can't clearly recall the way you smelled? Or whether or not you were easy to put to bed at night? Or what you said each morning when I'd get you from your crib...

. . . blink

Now...you are a medium—girl, just between childhood and the preteen thing. You feed yourself, clothe yourself, and most importantly, you think for yourself. I forget how fast this little journey is going. I forget that I won't remember the smell of your hair, or the way you collect notebooks, or how much you love Cheetos and Neopets and Pollys. This is my reminder to keep my eyes a little more open and my pen handy. To remember what can happen in a blink.

dear internet, today I...

Weblogs, or blogs, are the new diaries; they're personal, digital slices of life. And the fun part is that anyone can have one. It's another way to practice writing and getting more comfortable with how you express yourself through words.

I started blogging in March of 2005. Some of my friends were doing it, and initially I thought, "How cool is this? My own web site, and I don't even have to know how to design a web site."

What I didn't realize was how it would propel me into the habit of writing something every few days. Not only that, but the things I was putting out there could be used on my scrapbook pages.

Blogging can help you to be a more careful observer and reporter of your life. That's what it's done for me.

IS BLOGGING FOR YOU?

Whether it's to keep a cyber connection to distant family and friends, or to ponder the question "Am I an aging hipster?" blogs force you to do one thing: write something. Anything.

You serve as your own editor. Whatever you're comfortable putting out there, well, that's what you write about.

My own blog is a reflection of me in many ways. Mostly, I write about my latest obsessions—from music to food to whatever. Occasionally, I write about scrapbooking. But whatever I choose to say, it's coming from the gut. And the heart.

There are many blogging services you can check out (see Stuff I'm Recommending, p. 154). Think of them as writing aids for scrapbookers. Remember, the more you write, the more comfortable you'll get with it, and the easier it will be to write come journaling time.

THEN & NOW

20 years have come and passed, but the question remains: **am I an aging hipster?**

1. Had really great hair.	1. Had really great hair.
2. In heavy rotation: Duran Duran, Howard Jones, The Smiths, Bauhaus and Prince.	2. In heavy rotation: Green Day, Foo Fighters, Keane, Ben Harper and Peter Gabriel.
3. Typical friday night: drive down to Seattle, dance the night away at Skoochies, and try your very best to look really cool, even at the expense of being comfortable.	3. Typical friday night: break up fights between kids, watch reruns of *Making the Band 3*, put on PJs at 7 p.m. and actually *be* comfortable.
4. Make up routine: lots of heavy black eyeliner and use of excessive hair product.	4. Make up routine: manage to get a shower in and use of excessive hair product.
5. Think you are much cooler than everyone else.	5. Think you are much more tired than everyone else.
6. Think boys who wear a lot of heavy eye make up are hopelessly adorable.	6. Wish your hubby would have worn heavy black eyeliner to the Green Day concert.
7. Feel like, even at 19, you know a little something about life and how to live it.	7. Feel like, even at 39, you know a little something about life and how to live it.

INSPIRED BY BLOGGING

When I found the old shot you see above, and combined it with the fact that I was, at 39, headed off to a Green Day concert that night, it prompted me to blog about whether or not I was, in the words of the *Austin Powers* character Dr. Evil, "an aging hipster." I'd had an amusing conversation earlier in the day with a package clerk at the grocery store. He was excited about a concert he was going to, and when we realized we were both going to the same show, his reaction was initially shock, and then, "Whoa! That's so cool." Which I translated to mean: "Whoa! Even old people like cool music?"

I decided to pull out a recent photo and compare/contrast my hipster status today versus 20 year ago. I think the results speak for themselves. I really am a geek. But a geek with good hair, nonetheless.

the writer's notebook

All writers need a place to play. A place to jot, record, doodle, muse and highlight. That place is a writer's notebook, and you guessed it: scrapbookers need one, too!

I want you to start keeping a writer's notebook. I keep a few of them. One is for random layout ideas that pop into my head. One is for random journaling ideas. And the third is just to write about anything that's on my mind, whenever the mood strikes.

The one I use most is my little layout idea book. Different from a sketchbook, this little Moleskine journal is used solely to jot down layout content ideas, in the hopes that one day I'll get around to making that layout. There are times when a layout idea hits me—something that I think, "Man, I really want to do a page about that." And I'll write it down in my little journal. I may not get to it for months, but at least the idea is there for the taking.

The more you get into the habit of writing, the more "normal" writing will seem. Get a blank notebook and use it. To get into the habit of using it every day, commit to what I call the Two-Week High-Low Writing Challenge. Here's what you do:

At the end of each day, for a period of two weeks, write two things in your notebook: the best moment of your day and the worst moment of your day.

Now, keep in mind, these "high-low" moments may seem pretty ordinary at first, but what it forces you to do is think in terms of extremes every day. What was good? And what was bad? Then write four or five sentences describing each day's high and each day's low.

At the end of two weeks, you will have written something personal every day—something completely about you and your life experience. This is what "real" writers do. They get comfortable writing about what they know first. Then, they put their practice to work at their craft. You will do the same; you'll use the practice to become a better storyteller of your own life.

Don't be afraid that writing will get the best of you. Instead, let it *capture* the best of you. Be yourself. Practice. And just let it flow.

MAKE IT PERSONAL

I love my little Moleskine journal. It's cute, tiny and fits into my purse. I slapped the letter Z on it, and voila, it's a customized writer's notebook. Have a little fun. Pick up your own Moleskine journal, or some other blank book, and embellish it to suit your taste and style. Then, and here's the really important part: use it. Write in it. Keep it secret. Or share it with anyone who'll listen. Just start jotting things down when they hit you. If they never appear on a layout, that's okay. A writer's notebook is a place to write. If it becomes a source of scrapbook journaling inspiration, then more power to you. If not, it's still a valuable document about your life. In the end, that is what writing is all about.

a

sassy

i am ever glad, and ever joyed, and ever blessed, and ever everything...that you are my girl

design

Design is my life—well, a good chunk of it anyway. As a graphic

designer, my goal is to communicate, inform, educate and possibly

even entertain. Sounds a lot like scrapbooking, doesn't it? Reviewing

basic principles of design helps you keep developing your skill as a

scrapbooker. The more skilled you become, the easier your pages are

to put together. And visually, they won't look like a big pile of mucky

muck. You following me here? Good. Let's talk about design.

achieving balance

I could talk about design for an entire book. But I'm trying to present a more well-rounded picture of scrapbooking than just making pretty pages. That said, I won't lie: good design is critical to creating layouts that make visual sense. And the key to good design is balance.

To really understand balance, you have to understand space. Space is what you start with. And space can be a little bit intimidating, right? Those big, blank sheets of cardstock staring you right in the eye, challenging you: come on lady, bring it!

Achieving balance is simply taking control of space. It's like working a puzzle that's never been done before. You find spaces to fill with various pieces in a way that is logical and proportioned.

I'm going to share with you some approaches to achieving balance on your pages. And here's the secret: almost every principle of design contributes to creating balance. It's just a matter of working the puzzle until you get it right.

The pressure was on. I knew Molly would be wanting some great shots of her girlie, Anne, and it was my job to deliver. What I didn't expect was, that every time I pointed the camera in her direction, she would either say, "CHEESE!" with a big old forced grin, or make faces. After awhile though, she seemed to forget I was there, and I did manage to get a few good ones. But I still think the pouty shots are pretty darned cute, too. It was very cool to spend time with Molly, Gordie and Anne. Every now and then, you just need shots of someone else's kids. Especially ones with gorgeous blue eyes. So much easier to get the catchlight, isn't it?

pout

NOV. 2005

EVEN STEVEN

The layouts on these two pages are symmetrically balanced. The space on either side of the layout (above) or the spread (left) is occupied equally. Even with a few random embellishments and different photo sizes tossed in, the overall space is balanced and symmetrical.

Most of the pages I do are symmetrically balanced. Why? Because it guides me quickly to a finished result. When I know I'm going to fill a given space equally, it's as if there is an imaginary sketch that is telling me what to

do: the space I have filled on one side should also be filled on the other. What I put into that space doesn't matter as long as the space is filled equally.

On the "Two" layout, it doesn't matter that one side of the layout has a title and flower, and the other just photos. What you see as a whole are proportioned shapes of equal visual weight. The result is a symmetrically balanced layout.

You are five. Still. And I love this age. I love the things you say and do. Like when Miss K. was talking about Dr. Martin Luther King's legacy, and you said to her, "Why do the good die young?" Or when you tell Daddy, "I hope you brought your A game." Your mind is a miraculous little thing. And it really is still little. I have a hard time believing when I snuggle next to you at story time that you will ever be a full-grown boy. And when you become that boy, will you still let me hug you, and smell your skin, and kiss your cheeks? I love that you are five. I wish I could delay your next birthday by years. But I'm certain, I would miss out on how much I will love you at six, and seven, and beyond. I've just been feeling sort of sentimental lately, where you are concerned, my Coley. I just wanted to write it down. JANUARY 2005

FILLING SPACE UNEQUALLY

Asymmetry is created when you have something on one part of a given space, and the stuff on the other part is different. Different, but not random and haphazard.

The layout above is asymmetrical, because if you draw a line down the center of the page, the photos and the title combined carry more visual weight than the journaling.

The "Play" layout to the right is more clearly asymmetrical. The title is shifted off to the right,

the photos are different sizes, and there is a bit of extra white space above the journaling block. The two sides aren't mirror images.

One of the keys to the feel of balance here are the equal margins around the photos, title and patterned paper. Read more about margins on page 78.

12 kids aged six and under. Two coaches who have never really played soccer in their lives and happen to be Cole's parents. Fights over who gets to play goalie. Assorted crying jags every time someone gets called out for a substitute break. Trying to explain that they aren't in trouble, but that all the kids need a chance to play. Skinned knees and bumped craniums. Running around on crisp fall mornings, learning the game of soccer. Yep, that pretty much sums up Cole's first year on the team.

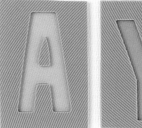

PLAY

39 pounds soaking wet
constantly talking, constantly moving
brave enough to get partially wet
the richest of imaginations
a finicky palette
the soul of a rock star
loved beyond measure

{six}

ANY WAY YOU SLICE IT

With asymmetrical design, balance is created by mixing and matching different elements, like titles, journaling, giant silk flowers and whatever else you want to put on the page.

The design can be a little bit looser with an asymmetrical approach. Use contrasting sizes and shapes to create energy and visual interest. Shift the majority of elements off to one side. Use one big photo, paired with several smaller ones. Play up the differences between elements.

If you're concerned about things going all willy nilly, here's a tip: leave a uniform margin of space on the outer edges of the layout. This creates a visual cushion to house and frame your page elements. For more on margins, turn the page.

On the layout above, the space above and below the photo are the same. The space to the left of the photo is similar to the space surrounding the letter sticker title. Even though all of these elements are different, they are held together by common margins of space, thereby enhancing the overall balance.

minneapolis
saintpaul
the place i call home

home

Growing up in Washington, I don't think I could have found Minneapolis on a map if I tried. I knew it was a some cold place in the middle of the country, and they had a football team called the Vikings. If I had only known then what Minneapolis and Saint Paul really, truly were, or were going to be...

It would be the place where I would marry my soul mate, and become part of a larger family of amazing people. It would be the place where my career in the creative arts would blossom. It would be the place where I brought two incredible other human beings into the world. It would be the place that I felt joy greater than any I'd every known, as well as a place where I would know sorrow and loss. It would be the place, essentially, of my life.

For 14 years I've called Saint Paul home, and although there are times I yearn for the mountains and oceans of Washington, I have realized that any place is home when you fill it with love. Even with its six-month long winters, there is no warmer place on Earth, to me. It's the place I call "home."

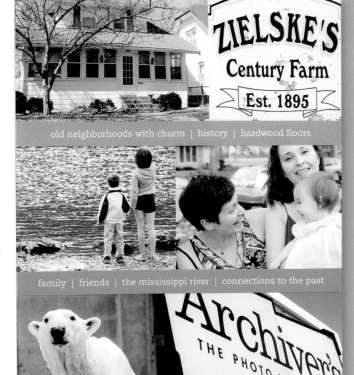

old neighborhoods with charm | history | hardwood floors

family | friends | the mississippi river | connections to the past

the como park zoo | saint's games | great shopping :)

THE MAGAZINE APPROACH

One of my favorite approaches to creating asymmetry is to take the magazine approach to design. Most magazine feature articles start on a two-page spread. There is usually a large visual on one of the pages, with the introduction to the article on the facing page. One big visual punch, supported by the text that begins the article.

If you told me I could never do another type of layout again, I would be happy doing this kind of scrapbook page every single time. I'm not kidding.

What's so cool about it is that you can do a large photo collage on one side, incorporating as many pictures as you like, and use all the room on the facing page to tell the story. And you can have as much white space on the journaling page as you like. The photo side of the spread serves as the anchor. It doesn't matter which side you choose for the photos, although I tend to put them on the right.

Of course, to do this, you're going to have to be comfortable with white space. Trust me, I have no shortage of praise for the value of white space. Next page, please.

margins and space

I'm going to propose a statement, and you may or may not agree, but chances are, if you're reading this book, you do:

Cathy makes really nice scrapbook pages.

Now if you do, in fact, agree, I'm going to tell you the number one reason they look nice, and the design convention that makes this possible: common margins. That's it. My secret is officially out. Most of my layouts incorporate equal margin space between visual elements. It's not just about being a linear, streamlined scrapbooker. It's about creating a cushion of color to hold all of the elements on the page. That cushion is the background cardstock. The equalization of margin space is the glue that holds everything together. Makes sense, right?

I don't actually measure the margins. It's just eyeball work. But it gives me a way to piece together the layout puzzle and provide one strong unifying element: the background.

Equal margin spaces are really just small areas of white space (areas with nothing in them) that serve to unify the whole layout. Incorporating common margins into your page designs will make you say to this to yourself: *I make really nice scrapbook pages.*

four girls sleeping over | rockin' robin clap thingies | strictly ballroom and popcorn | silly games with daddy | no major spats | sleeping bags on the floor | lights out at midnight | actual sleep at roughly 2 a.m. | hope you had a happy birthday, boots

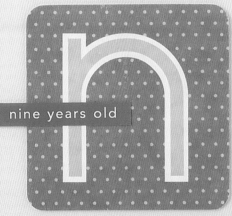

nine years old

THE RULES OF MARGINS

Make them equal in width. That's the only rule. However, notice on this layout that the patterned paper on the left side runs right to the edge? I did it on purpose, because I wanted it to subtly link the number "9" that runs off the edge. Then notice that the margin between the left edge of the page and the start of the journaling block is the same as the other margins. Yep. Did that on purpose, too.

A WORD ABOUT SPACE

Just as I like a clean house with little clutter (an impossibility when you factor in the pack rats I live with), I also like a clean layout with less stuff and more space.

White space is about letting what you have to show and say stand on its own. It's about the drama of a good photo shining in all its glory. It's about giving the eye a much needed rest. It's about purity of intent. It's a calm in the storm of visual life.

For some scrapbookers, it's hard not to fill up every space on a layout with stuff. I get that. I really do. But I also know that a lot of scrapbookers want to achieve a timeless quality to their work. There is nothing more timeless than simplicity. Incorporating white space is the ultimate exercise in visual simplification.

Try a few pages with a lot of space. If it's really killing you to not fill it up, then go ahead. I won't be knocking on your door to see if you've made the official white space quota. But I'll bet you a package of paper flowers—one that you will use oh-so sparingly—that you might surprise yourself with how much you like the results.

RED FISH, BLUE FISH...

White space doesn't have to be white. It can be any color you're scrapping on, as long as it's empty.

conduct

NOVEMBER 2005

A field trip with 60 kindergartners is guaranteed to do two things: one, remind you that five and six year olds see the world with passion and enthusiasm long since forgotten by grown ups; and two, give you yet another reason to thank the makers of Advil. That said, there was another "thing" that resulted from this outing to the Minnesota Wildlife Refuge Center: intense pride.

Coley, watching the way you conduct yourself in a group made me so incredibly proud to be your mother. Your politeness. The way you follow the rules. The way you participate in everything. The way you watched the short film and could hardly contain the answer to the question of who began the National Wildlife Refuge Programs (and yes, you were the only kid in the room to answer, "Roosevelt!") I know it's not all parenting, but I feel like maybe your Dad and I are doing something right. You are such a genuinely nice young man, with zeal and passion. I'm incredibly proud of who you are, and continue to become.

one
tough
hombré

See the problem is the big old grin. Oh sure, you can pull the

tough kid thing off for a few minutes at a time, but to suppress

that impish grin is nearly impossible. For the record—you picked

out the costume and head gear for this shot. All I wanted was to

try out my new camera and shoot some nice portraits. I got this.

And you know what? I like your approach better.

APRIL 2, 2004

groups are good

Unity—a critical principle of graphic design—is achieved when elements in a given space have a direct, cohesive relationship to one another.

When I make scrapbook pages, it's really hard for me to think of anything in isolation. It's all about the overall flow. How do the elements tie together? Grouping photos together into one large "block" of images is one way I create a unified relationship on my pages.

When photos are unified, it's easy to know where to look first for your visual information. Rather than randomly placing photos on a page, these four photos below are grouped together in a shared, common space.

COME TOGETHER, RIGHT NOW

Grouping photos together is one of the best ways to create a unified look and feel on any page. Groups create a strong visual cue: look right here for the pictures! Butting photos up against one another without any margin space is a simple way to group them together. The "Homework" layout on the right, with just two photos, does this. The visual information is linked. You can take it in all at once. Don't make people hunt for the visual information (your photos)!

HOMEWORK

discover

5

Twelve more years of it, Buddy—and that isn't counting college! I know, it seems a titch unfair to make 5-year-olds do homework, but so it goes. You bring home a homework folder each Thursday. And then, you plug away. You're already up to the letter "i"! What could be next? J? Keep working hard, Coley. A great student, you'll be.

{studio envy}

LIFT THIS DESIGN

This layout is one of the first pages I did after getting back into the 12 x 12 game. I plan to lift it over and over, because I think it's a page with potential. There are seven "live" spaces to work in. You can mix and match journaling, embellishments and photos however you like in those spaces. So all you scrappers who want to get more photos on a page, but still keep it clean, use this as a template for your next layout.

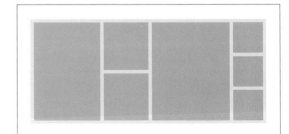

Studio envy. Something that has cropped up—no pun intended—with alarming frequency of late. I know, I know...I should be completely thankful that I have a dedicated space at all. But the other night, while I was curling up with a recent issue of *CK*, the one with the top 10 lists, I found myself turning a little green as I peeked into the "studios" of all those scrapbookers. ¶ I began to dream of what it would be like to have an actual studio—not just a part-time dining room; one where you can hang excess product on the walls; one where you can spread it out and leave it out; one where you can sound really pretentious when you say, *"Want to see my studio?"* ¶ I have this secret plan that Dan doesn't know about. It's the plan where we build onto the back of the house—where the deck is currently—and create my dream studio. It would have a half-wall separating it from the family room, and I could watch *Oprah* from a short distance, while creating and playing. (Actually, I could watch Nickelodeon. Getting to watch *Oprah*...let's get back to reality here.) I would have a custom-built table, sort of like the work table we used to have at the Science Museum. At least 10 feet long, with flat files on one side, for works in progress, and cubbies galore. Then there would be custom cabinets, with shelving for all the cardstock, and patterned paper. I would paint the room a really lovely pink, or green. I would order some vinyl cut letters from WonderfulWords.com that said, "take more naps" and put that on the wall. There would be windows on the south and the west. Glorious natural light everywhere. ¶ I know, I know...I shouldn't want what I cannot have. But it doesn't hurt to dream, right? Think I'll head up to SA...there are a few lottery tickets with my name on them.

ONE BIG CANVAS

Think of your two-page spread as one large canvas. These aren't two 12 x 12 pages; they are one 24 x 12 page. Everything is grouped together, with an ample cushion of white space framing the visual content.

make a visual statement

One big picture, paired with several smaller pictures, will always equal one thing: one fine scrapbook page with great visual interest. We're talking about the design principle of contrast. Contrast can be created easily through the use of size. Something is really big; the other things are much smaller. Simple, right?

In scrapbook page design, big stuff can make an impact, engaging our sense of sight and piquing our curiosity.

The other cool thing about using big photos to create contrast is that if you're making 8½ x 11 pages, one enlarged photo can become an entire page. Like the opening of a magazine article, it communicates the topic of your "spread."

Here: the first day of school for a kid who is clearly too little to be going off in a school bus for the first time. The photo says as much to me as the words do.

FIND THE FOCAL POINT

Not too hard, is it? One of the easiest ways to create a dominant focal point is by using enlarged photos. Notice how your eye lands on the big shot first, the smaller shots second and the journaling third? That's called visual hierarchy. The eye is directed by descending order of size.

coleman's first day of school   9.09.04

firstday

I didn't even have time to cry. It all happened so fast. There were kids, and parents, and everyone was talking about the first day of school and before I knew it, I was giving you a final, rushed hug and kiss…and then you were off. During the preceding weeks, you were growing increasingly more apprehensive about the start of school. I really wasn't sure how that first morning would unfold. Would you refuse to get out of bed? Would you dissolve into a sobbing heap as the bus pulled up? Or would the sobbing heap be me? As I said, it all happened so fast, even though we were at the bus stop a full half an hour before it actually arrived. You were excited to get on with it—take that next step in your childhood, which, by my watch, is flying by at super sonic speed. It all happened so fast. One minute, you are an hour old, nestled safely in my arms where nothing in this entire world could ever harm you. And the next minute, you're climbing onto a school bus, with a back pack almost as big as you are, heading off and away from me. I may now have found the time to cry, baby boy, but it's a mixed bag of sadness, pride, memory and hope. Good luck, buddy. You'll do just fine. And so will I.

The greatest day in your life was the day Daddy took you to Play It Again Sports and picked up mismatched, second-hand catcher gear. Yes, that's right—the greatest day in your then, five years. You came home, you put it on, you could barely move, and you were the happiest boy in the world. You've got gear. Doesn't really matter if you can even play. October 2004

SPEAKING OF ENLARGEMENTS...

Without question, the 5 x 7 photo is the perfect size for scrapbooking. It fits nicely all by itself on a page, or it serves as the natural focal point on a two-page spread. Because enlargements are pretty cheap, the next time you're getting photos printed, pick a few shots and get some 5 x 7s to play with.

Whether they fill a good chunk of an 8½ x 11 page or look elegantly spare on a 12 x12, 5 x 7s are super versatile.

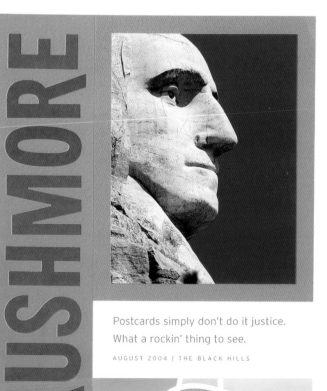

RUSHMORE

Postcards simply don't do it justice.
What a rockin' thing to see.

AUGUST 2004 | THE BLACK HILLS

SCENES FROM OUR SUMMER ROAD TRIP

SiLLY LUKEY POSING FOR THE CAMERA, AUGUST 2005 **GOOFY** PHOTO FROM OUR WEEKEND CAMPING TRIP

ROOM TO PLAY

Initially, I was worried that putting a 5 x 7 photo in the
center of this layout would make it seem too small. But it
allowed me room to add the patterned paper squares and
chipboard letters, which filled in the space more fully.

can you do that again?

Repetition makes scrapbook pages make more sense. How? Repeated things—sizes, embellishments, colors or shapes—feel comfortable and predictable. Our brains try to make sense of things by figuring out how they are connected. When we see things repeated, a visual path is created that helps us connect the dots and interpret what we see.

Repetition also creates a sort of a rhythm; a subtle, or not so subtle, set of visual punctuation marks on a page. You can repeat anything, and this is good news for scrapbook product manufacturers. Why use one of something when you

can use three, or five, or more? But it's not just product. You can repeat color, shape and photo sizes. And don't forget techniques. On my "Girls' Weekend" layout, I inked the edges of all the cardstock. That's a simple, repeated technique that ties the layout together.

Repeating elements contribute to the overall balance of a page. The circle stickers below balance one another and link the two-page spread with repeated shapes. Repetition is really that simple. Find stuff. Repeat it.

SHAPE AND COLOR

You can repeat colors and shapes just as easily as embellishments. Here, long thin strips of cardstock are repeated (shape) as well as the colors. I repeated a bit more brown by using a brown pen and brad.

I also repeated this photo! I used it on another layout back on page 24. If you love a photo, there's no rule that says you can't scrapbook it more than once.

summer time

blowing bubbles

swimsuits and sunscreen

THE MAGIC NUMBER THREE

Repeating an element three times is optimum. Odd numbers of elements have slightly more energy than even numbers. Think of the difference between symmetrical (formal, stable) and asymmetrical (informal, energized). This also applies to the number of times an element is repeated. My friend Donna has a cute kid, who, as you may notice above, has been repeated in photographs three times.

On the "Reflect" layout, I repeated the floral pattern and the polka dot pattern three times. Further, the brads, while even in total number, are grouped in three locations. And the floral pattern is in what is called a visual triangle. A visual triangle is when you place three elements on a page, and they form a triangular relationship to one another.

Something seems to be missing lately. That thing is scrapbooking. I dont know if its the digital camera factor, in that, i no longer have stacks of photos that i can flip through, or if its simply a general lack of motivation. I just know i'm not really taking the time to record our lives. And i miss it. Maybe i just need a little break from time to time. Maybe through the course of my blogging, I'm running out of stories to tell, or things to say. Whatever the case may be, i need to stop and take the time. Maybe i just need to pick some events and get them down. I just am missing playing with paper and glue. And therein lies the message of this page. 5.22.05

reflect /ri-'flekt/ verb
1. to look back upon the past with fondness
2. reminisce

memories

IDEAS FROM PATTERNED PAPER

Patterned paper is a great resource for choosing color schemes to repeat on a layout. Orange, lavender and lime green are triadic—they sit equidistant from one another on the color wheel. In theory, I should know all of the possible harmonious color wheel combinations; the truth is, I don't. I think paper manufacturers are fabulous at giving us color schemes for the taking. Just match up a few shades of cardstock to your pattern and scrap!

Be sure to repeat the same colors in die cuts or embellishments (in threes!) and lettering.

designing good type

Although I achieved a scrapbooking milestone this year by embracing my handwriting, my first love still lies with the gazillion fonts on my Mac's hard drive. I'm a font lover. User. Addict.

Type is part of the reason I got so hooked on this hobby. I've worked as a graphic designer for many years, and when I made the connection that I could use my skills as a typographer to make pretty scrapbook pages, I knew I'd found a hobby that would let me be me.

I get asked a lot of questions about type: How do I organize fonts? Where do I get fonts? How do I make type run up the side of the page? How do I set type in a circle? What fonts are best to use?

Rather than dole out step-by-step processes, I like to focus on theoretical type scenarios first, and throw in a few tricks later. If you know how type works, on principle, then the rest is just technological tinkering.

So let's start with some type basics—some solid information to get you thinking about type and how to take control of it and make it work for you.

Guitar. Bass. Drums. For some reason, as I stare down the barrel of 40, I'm going back to my roots, listening to the kind of music I was into at 15. Rock and roll. Loud. Raunchy. Raucous. Did I mention loud? Yes, I confess. I was a new wave junkie. I had my share of Duran Duran, and Howard Jones, and all that great '80s music and hair. Then my so-called "intelligent" music phase: R.E.M., Tom Waits, The Sundays, and so on and so forth. I listened to the bands I was supposed to listen to. That whole thing. And now? It's just back to straight rock and roll. From Green Day to Foo Fighters, to AC/DC and Led Zep. It must somehow be hard-wired into my system from all that teen-aged rocking. Once that guitar solo starts, I'm putty...rock and roll putty.

CONTRAST IS KING

Something big. Something small. This is one approach to creating a title with a strong visual punch. The word "rock" is set to 150 points, while the words "and roll" are set to 50 points. There is no magical, perfect equation to create the ultimate type contrast. It involves a little bit of trial and error until it feels right.

Sometimes the best way to learn what works and what doesn't is to imitate type you see in the world at large. You don't need to know exactly what typeface someone used to create something that mimics it.

Just remember that making one word big looks really cool, and doing it isn't all that difficult.

I resolve

2006

to work a little less and
play a little more

to think a bit longer
before I speak

to move my body more
than I do now

to listen better

to keep playing my guitar, no
matter how bad it sounds

to embrace my gifts

to be happy with less

to be thankful for what
I have, every day

ONE TYPEFACE

This layout uses one typeface: Interstate. It's always a good
idea to invest in one, classic typeface with numerous
weights. It gives you tons of options within a single font.

leading, spacing and columns

Sometimes, you will have a lot to say. And you'll use type to say it. And you'll end up with a ton of really clever words and phrases to tell your amazing story.

Just do me one favor: break it up. Avoid making one giant text box that spans the width of your page. While it may look fine from a visual standpoint, I can guarantee you it will be hard to read. If one of your goals in scrapbooking your life is to share it with others, try to make it easier on their eyes. Break up your long journaling sections into columns. Or make sure your journaling block isn't wider than four inches, five at the most. The rule of thumb should be: the wider your column of text, the larger your leading should be (the vertical space between the lines of text).

The layout at right is pretty text heavy. But by keeping my column width to 3½ inches, combined with a nice amount of leading (22 points), I doubt reading it will give you a headache.

WHAT'S WRONG WITH THE LAYOUT BELOW?
One word: italics. Why I decided to journal in the italic version of this particular font, I'll never know. The only thing that saves this huge amount of text is leading, columns and spacing. But trust me, your eyes will be hurting. A good example of do as I say, not as I do.

he wants to be, your

SLEDGEHAMMER

My son has an obsession. His name is Peter Gabriel. And I, for one, couldn't be any more tickled about it! It all started last fall when, after seeing Mr. Gabriel in concert, I came home and decided to order a concert film called "Secret World Live" from the tour I'd missed in 1994. I popped it into the VCR and voilá— a new idol, in Coley's eyes, was born. It started out simply enough—he just wanted to watch the "Steam" segment over and over. He would stand in front of the television, and mimic every move that Peter did on stage. But then, it began to change. He wanted to know who the guitar player was. Who was the bass player? What was the drummer's name? Who's the guy with the violin? Then, he decided to watch a little more. Soon, "Kiss that Frog" and "Solisbury Hill" were added to his mix of requests. Before I knew it, Coley was watching the entire tape from beginning to end, singing and dancing along with Peter and his band. But it doesn't stop there. No, now it's much more serious. I picked up another concert film called, "PoV" from 1986, and now, Coley will either request Old Peter or New Peter.

Now he's learning all sorts of new songs, like "Shock the Monkey," and "Biko," the song about the late South African human rights activist Steven Biko. And Coley is so emphatic when he joins in for the chanting portion at the end of the song (as seen in the pictures to the right.) It's hard to capture just how involved Coley is with Peter right now. When "Secret World" comes on, Coley spins in circles, and makes all the music sounds with his mouth while wielding his baseball bat [read "guitar"] as he emulates the riffs by PG's guitarist David Rhodes. I mean, come on, how many three year olds can sit at the breakfast table and sing "Digging in the Dirt?" I ask you! How many? How many know the full name's of any musical artist's touring band? And makes his family play all the different band members? Suffice to say it's a heck of a lot more enjoyable that watching Barney videos all day long. My Coley, you are as entertaining as the day is long. And I will watch Peter Gabriel with you anytime you want.

JANUARY 2003

THIS WILL BE MY TESTIMONY, YEAH...YEAH!

my
favorite
room

1.05

This morning, while plugging away on Donna's book projects, all alone in a quiet house, save for the Peter Gabriel DVD that was playing on my second monitor, I realized this: I love my office! For such a long time, this room was a haphazard jumble of stuff that never made any sense from a Feng Shui point of view. And then, I went to IKEA.

For just under $600, I transformed the space into my perfect little office. A new credenza, created from two IKEA buffet bottoms. A new bookcase and matching CD case for more stuff. And, some frames and other little chachki stuff to make me happy. Happy, inspired, relaxed…and ready to work.

I realized how much my space, and being happy in it, contributes to my overall flow as a designer. It's everything. When I'm surrounded by space and stuff that makes sense, I make things look better. And better looking things are good.

I love the whole gig. Working from home, in my ratty old orange sweatshirt and torn up cargo pants. No makeup. Listening to a Prince CD on iTunes and my Harmon-Kardon speakers, three times in a row, just because I'm feeling the groove. This is my space. This is my work. I couldn't dig it anymore than I do. I'm pretty dang lucky.

I may not have the elusive custom scrap room, and believe me, there are times when I get the itch to try and convince Dan that this office should become just that. Then I realize that my space for the real work that I do needs to be dedicated and focused. That, is how I work best.

It's official—the office is my favorite room. In here, I'm at home, refreshed, and ready to work, connect or play. You can't beat that with a stick.

PLEASE SIR, COULD I HAVE A BIT MORE SPACE?
Don't be afraid to break up your journaling into separate paragraphs.
It adds a little bit of restful space that enhances readability.

CREATING COLUMNS

Here's how to do it in Microsoft Word: Create a text box as wide as you'd like your column to be. Follow this path under the Insert menu:

Insert > Text Box

Use the side handles to drag the height and width to your liking, and type away.

The simplest way to make a second column is to copy and paste your first text box, and continue typing over the existing text. You'll have to make sure your sentences flow from the end of one box to the next. There! A quick and easy way to make columns.

TAKE CONTROL OF LEADING

Promise me this: you will no longer rely on the default leading set up by your word processing program. You will take control and set your own, custom leading for your journaling blocks. Agreed?

It's this easy. Type your journaling. Go to **Format > Paragraph**. Select the **Indents and Spacing** tab. In the **Spacing** option, select **Exact**, and enter a number that is four to six points larger than your type size (see chart on facing page).

This will give you a nice amount of space and make your words much easier to read. Don't be afraid to experiment a bit. Make your leading amount really big to see how different your text will look.

And one final plea. Remember, when typing, just one space after a period. Please? Okay? Don't create weird gaps of space between your sentences.

Since the day you arrived, I've let you go at your own pace. No charts or measurements or new word counts. No concerns about when you should be doing this, or that. I quit my job to enjoy being your mother. There were no rules, and no limits. Just you—glorious you—and time.

So why is it, that on the eve of the start of Kindergarten, I'm feeling like somewhere along the way, I broke my end of the deal? Somewhere between scrapbooking and finding a new career direction, did I distract you one too many times with the T.V., or a new toy, or your box of Legos? Did I have to send one more e-mail, scrap one more assigned page, or meet one more deadline?

On more than one occasion during the past year, I've said how cool it's going to be when you are in school as an all-day friend. Oh, the work I'll get done! No more late nights and weekends. I can focus on being a mom the minute you walk in the door. I can't help but feel like that focus should've never shifted. Not from the minute your precious, irreplaceable soul landed on this earth. And I can't go back.

Tonight, your tears came fast and furious when I tucked you in. You didn't want to go tomorrow. The day would be too long. You didn't want to go to music class. You wouldn't be able to finish your lunch before the bell rang, so I shouldn't

pack you more than three things to eat. And as I tried to comfort you, and Aidan was offering her support as well, it just came out, in one soulful, sob-choked burst:

"I'm going to miss my Mom."

It was like an arrow to the heart. And I couldn't hide it from you. In all my imaginings, I never, ever thought I would hear that from the little boy who's been pushing the limits all summer long. Who's fought every bath. Who's been doing things his own way. Who's been asserting his growing independence.

I never stopped to think about the fact that he was going to miss me.

I wish I could bring back every peanut butter and jelly sandwich, and read you more stories, and play catch and baseball, and go for bike rides and all that stuff that *is* what becomes memory in a six-year-old mind.

I hope you know, Coley, how much I love you. How I hope. How I hope.

I'm going to miss my son.

HOW MUCH LEADING?

I start with the following guides and adjust from there. Remember, over time, you'll begin to develop an eye for what looks right.

TYPE SIZE	LEADING
10	18
12	22
14	28

tips and tricks for type

Generally speaking, I don't like type tricks. I'm a purist at heart. I'd much rather see you create a beautiful journaling block, with ample leading (and only one space after a period!) than see you set type inside a circle or make it look 3-D. But that's just me. I'm typographically boring.

I believe that's why my type looks good on pages. I keep the tricks to a minimum. Keep the typographic bells and whistles on the down low, if you get my drift. Keep it simple.

There are only a couple of type techniques you need to know to start making an impact and having more control over how everything comes together, such as changing type color (including white), and overlapping elements. All can be done in Microsoft Word.

A little restraint goes a long way. Keep it simple and make an impact.

REVERSE TYPE

A color printer, cardstock or photo paper, and the ability to change the color of your type to white is all you need to create the reverse type effect. In Word, simply choose a background color for your text box, and then highlight your text and change its color to white. To change the background color of a text box, simply double-click on the edge of the box to bring up **Format Text Box**. Select **Lines and Fill**, and choose a **Fill** color. For creating a custom color, see the sidebar on the next page.

CUSTOM COLOR

The easiest way to create a custom color for type or background is to use the color picker wheel. To get to the color picker in Word, follow this pathunder the **Format** menu: **Font > Font Color > More Colors**. Click anywhere in the wheel to find your color. Then use the slider on the side to deepen or lighten the hue. It took me two tries to get the "@" symbol the right shade of green.

UNDERSTANDING THE PICKER

This is the color picker in Word. Once you have the picker displayed, move the slider on the right-hand side up and down. Notice how it changes the color values? You can select a point anywhere on the wheel itself, and then move the slider to alter the color. You'll see the results in the upper bar at the top of the window. If you find a color you like, click once in the bar and drag down to the lower palette of colors, beneath the wheel. The color will then be part of your permanent library of color.

On most scrapbook pages, I journal first and add everything else later. Why? First, I want to have room for the story. And second, if I know how large my journaling box is, I can build the rest of the layout to fit accordingly.

But you can also get a perfectly fitted journaling box if you work in reverse—pictures and embellishments first. Just measure the space where you want your journaling to go, and create a text box that size in Word. After you insert your text box, double click the edge of the box and select the **Size** tab. Enter the desired height and width, and then increase the size by one increment by using the up arrows to the right of each measurement box. Keep the line option for your text box, and when you print it out, use that line as your trim guide, cutting just to the inside of the line. This should give you a pretty close match to the original size you were shooting for.

The first day of an entirely new era: the 4th grade. It marks a big step for you, Aidan. No longer at the top of the food chain in E1, now, you're moving onto E2, into a class with fifth and sixth graders. I know intellectually you'll have no problems at all. I hope that you are able to adjust to your new surroundings with ease. Fifth and sixth graders can be a little intimidating at first. But, I think with your confidence and social skills, you'll be making an entirely new host of friends as you find your place in this new academic environment. Be yourself. Be open to change. But also, remember who you are. You are an amazing girl, with an engaging personality, a heart of gold and great instincts. Trust that, Boots, and you'll do just fine. SEPTEMBER 2005

tales of a fourth grade something a

OVERLAPPING TYPE

In Word, create two different text boxes (**Insert>text box**). Double click the edge of each box to remove both the **Line and Fill** options. Then, simply move one box over the other.

You can change the order of the text boxes as well. First, select the text box you want to affect. Next, go to the **View** menu and select the **Formatting Palette**. Proceed to the **Size, Rotation and Ordering** submenu in the **Formatting Palette**. The **Layering** option lets you move your text box forward or backward.

It also helps to change the color of the type you are layering, to achieve the desired effect.

really super cute. really loud. really creative. really smart. really good at getting what you want. really funny. really friendly. really good travelers. really play well with others. really original. really good ability to quote film dialogue, especially from the Austin Powers series. really brown eyes. really messy rooms. really unlimited potential. really cool parents, or so we think. really big meltdowns. really, really, really, really loved.

Z

05 | reallyzielske

THE FINAL WORD

Type can be simple if you let it be. One font. Varying weights. Varying sizes. You need nothing more. Truly. This layout? One font: Avenir, in varying weights. My favorite typefaces are: Times New Roman, Caecilia, Interstate and now, Avenir. They never look exactly the same to me, because every layout tells a different story, uses different photos and has a different design.

Learn what your go-to fonts are, the ones you feel most comfortable with, and then use them again and again. Unless of course, your go-to font is Comic Sans. Then, we need to talk.

Another cool thing about the layout above? Once I picked the color for the type, I created blank text boxes, filled them with the same colors, and printed them on white cardstock. Yes, it uses a lot of ink toner, but it's kind of fun to make custom-colored cardstock.

make

Enough with single layouts. It's time for the pièce de résistance

of simplicity—simple scrapbooks. One theme. One album.

One design. One cool process. You want vacation ideas?

Holiday ideas? Ideas for scrapbooking about paper towels?

Then settle in. I've got some things to show you.

please, not more vacation photos

It's been said that there is nothing more boring than someone else's travel photos. While I can attest to flipping through a stack or two of someone else's journeys with less than keen interest, I still believe that my own travel photos are highly scrapworthy.

My summer vacation of 2004 involved two things: one, a cross-country road trip hitting major American landmarks on the way to my 20-year high school reunion, and two, a new digital camera. Long story short: I took nearly 700 pictures of said landmarks, despite leaving home without the camera's battery charger.

(Read the journaling on the next few pages. My near nervous breakdown is well documented.)

Once I had narrowed it down to roughly 200 photos, my task was clear: I would create a simple scrapbook—a theme album—with a defined framework to help me organize and assemble all of this information.

But what exactly is a simple scrapbook? It is an album documenting a single, defined subject— in this case, my summer vacation. But simple scrapbooks can be about anything you want.

TITLE PAGE

what we did on our summer
VACATION

seattle or bust '04

What started out as a "hey, I think I will go to my 20-year high school reunion" evolved into a full-fledged family road trip to Seattle, Wash. Not just a straight shot there, but to wind our way through South Dakota, paying a visit to Mount Rushmore and Crazy Horse. Then onto the amazing thermal wonders of Yellowstone National Park. In short, see the country, courtesy of our Hyundai Santa Fe. So much to remember. Coley's new laugh. Hoards of Sturgis bikers. Heated slug bug competitions. The Athens 2004 Olympic Games. Aidan's immaculate courtesy. And spending time with dear and cherished friends. I love my road trippin' family. This is dedicated with love to the three people who put the "trip" into road trip. September 2004.

SETTING THE STAGE

I try to include a "Dedication" page in every theme album I create. It helps get my mojo flowing. I have a chance to introduce what's going to take place on the following pages.

SECTION PAGES

This summer one third of the nation will be ill-housed, ill-nourished, and ill-clad. Only they'll call it a vacation.

JOSEPH SALAK

MITCHELL CORN PALACE

LEWIS & CLARK 2004

the world-famous corn palace

MITCHELL

day number one

FILLER PAGES

DAY ONE
AUGUST 13, 2004

The adventure begins...we left on a friday afternoon on our grand adventure—the summer road trip to Seattle. With the car completely loaded, the requisite iPod and DVD selections in place, Goldfish, Slim Jims, cookies and other snack-foods to keep our energy up for the drive. You never really know how good Goldfish are until you're driving across the country with a bag of them in your lap!

Our day one destination—Mitchell, S.D. We pulled into the Mitchell Holiday Inn around dinner time, and it was off to the pool for the kids, and off to a little quiet time for Mom who made friends with Sturgis' bikers.

After dinner, we played 18 holes of miniature golf in the hotel, and then it was back to the room to get ready for bed. Running simultaneously with our trip was the 2004 Athens Summer Olympics. Thus began the nightly hotel tradition of watching the Olympics until we fell asleep.

The first day was a success. We kept it short and sweet. Would it be a sign of future driving days to come?

HIGHLIGHTS
AND LOWLIGHTS

It's hard to say whether or not the Corn Palace was a highlight. It's a building that is decorated in corn. You start seeing the billboards for it about 300 miles before you get there. They say things like, "Ears to you" and other clever corn-related turns of phrase. Once you get inside, it's just a photo gallery of the various eras of the palace and a huge tourist trap gift shop.

Yes, the kids learned a new term on this trip: tourist trap.

But the first mishap of the trip was huger than huge—of colossal proportion: my camera battery died and guess who forgot to bring her battery charger? Can you say, "We are headed to Mount Rushmore and can't take any pictures?" Can you also say, "Mom, you need to breathe now or you'll pass out?"

We decided to try our luck for a battery in Rapid City, S.D. Surely they would have one in stock, right? Yeah, Rapid City is a big town. It's just a little Nikon battery. Everyone has those.

ANATOMY OF A SIMPLE SCRAPBOOK

Simple scrapbooks contain all or some of the following elements:

TITLE PAGE

The title page sets the stage for your entire album. This is where you'll introduce your topic, your color scheme, your design, your embellishments—everything that's going to show up on the successive pages.

The title page often takes the longest to figure out. But this is always my first step when designing a theme album. Many times, I will repeat the design for my section pages. Why reinvent the wheel? Remember, this is *simple* scrapbooking.

DEDICATION PAGE

Who is this for, or what is this about? Dedications are actually my favorite part of a simple scrapbook. The dedication page is a place, not only to say who the book is for, but to recap and expound upon whatever it is that you are scrapbooking about. It's a place to have fun, be silly, be sincere—a place to simply "be yourself."

SECTION PAGES

These are the pages that divide up your album into sections. For my vacation album, each stop along the way is broken up into its own section. Section pages should have the same design repeated again and again for consistency. I simply took the same design used on my title page and repeated it.

DAY ONE
AUGUST 13, 2004

The adventure begins...we left on a friday afternoon on our grand adventure—the summer road trip to Seattle. With the car completely loaded, the requisite iPod and DVD selections in place, Goldfish, Slim Jims, cookies and other snack-foods to keep our energy up for the drive. You never really know how good Goldfish are until you're driving across the country with a bag of them in your lap!

Our day one destination—Mitchell, S.D. We pulled into the Mitchell Holiday Inn around dinner time, and it was off to the pool for the kids, and off to a little quiet time for Mom who made friends with Sturgis' bikers.

After dinner, we played 18 holes of miniature golf in the hotel, and then it was back to the room to get ready for bed. Running simultaneously with our trip was the 2004 Athens Summer Olympics. Thus began the nightly hotel tradition of watching the Olympics until we fell asleep.

The first day was a success. We kept it short and sweet. Would it be a sign of future driving days to come?

HIGHLIGHTS
AND LOWLIGHTS

It's hard to say whether or not the Corn Palace was a highlight. It's a building that is decorated in corn. You start seeing the billboards for it about 300 miles before you get there. They say things like, "Ears to you" and other clever corn-related turns of phrase. Once you get inside, it's just a photo gallery of the various eras of the palace and a huge tourist trap gift shop.

Yes, the kids learned a new term on this trip: tourist trap.

But the first mishap of the trip was huger than huge—of colossal proportion: my camera battery died and guess who forgot to bring her battery charger? Can you say, "We are headed to Mount Rushmore and can't take any pictures?" Can you also say, "Mom, you need to breathe now or you'll pass out?"

We decided to try our luck for a battery in Rapid City, S.D. Surely they would have one in stock, right? Yeah, Rapid City is a big town. It's just a little Nikon battery. Everyone has those...

The one variation I used was to create a section spread, with a quote about travel on the left-facing page. This is certainly not required, but I thought it added a cool visual element. And it provided a nice amount of breathing space to break up my photo-intensive scrapbook.

FILLER PAGES

Filler pages are where your journaling and photos go. Again, a consistent design will not only unify your album, it will make it easier for you to follow and complete. I took nearly 700 photos during this vacation. Now, because I'm not an insane person, I wasn't about to scrapbook all of them. After carefully editing my shots down to a manageable 200, I sorted them and started cutting and pasting.

There is very little "traditional" scrapbooking on these pages. I knew if I ever wanted to finish this album, I couldn't get all fancy. This meant no embellishments. Just journaling blocks and pictures. You don't have to have brads, paper flowers, die cuts and stickers on every page to make it qualify as a "scrapbook." If you have photos and words combined, you've succeeded.

CLOSING PAGE

A closing page, while a nice touch, is optional. Personally, I have yet to make a closing page for a theme album.

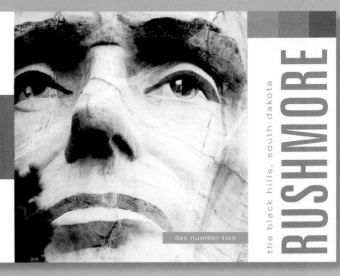

> Like all great travelers, I have seen more than I remember,
> and remember more than I have seen.
>
> BENJAMIN DISRAELI

the black hills, south dakota

RUSHMORE

day number two

DAY TWO
AUGUST 14, 2004

Long story short: Ritz Camera in Rapid City did have one Nikon battery in stock, but no charger. So, I figured I'd roll the dice, and hoped it lasted through Mount Rushmore. In the mean time, I called my neighbor, Sarah, and asked her to overnight my charger to Molly's house. Thank goodness I left her my house key!

Ah…now where were we? We pulled into Keystone, S.D. at around 4:30 p.m., swam, ordered a pizza, and decided to head out to see Mount Rushmore at sunset. The main street of Keystone was filled to capacity with bikes as far as the eye could see. Oh, Sturgis!

We headed up to see the famous mountain, and when it came into view, it was really quite awesome. Having never seen it before, I was just as excited as the kids.

We stayed for the evening lighting ceremony, which was preceded by a concert and a film about the women behind the presidents. It was such a peaceful, calm and beautiful night. We couldn't have custom-ordered anything better.

Mount Rushmore National Memorial

National Park Service
U.S. Department of the Interior

GUTZON BORGLUM
Sculpted by his son
Lincoln Borglum

The Power to Carve a Mountain

Over 450,000 tons of rock were removed from Mount Rushmore to bring out the four presidential faces. Although about about 90% of the rock was removed with dynamite, the remaining rock was removed by drilling with jackhammers and wedging the rock off the mountain. The final finishing work on the faces was completed using small jackhammers and facing bits. Air compressors located here at the base of the mountain were used to power the jackhammers. Electricity to power the compressors came from a power plant located at this

location during the carving work. For much of the life of the carving, Keystone Consolidated Mines provided the electrical power to operate these compressors.

An 1,800-foot, 3-inch pipeline followed the stairway up the mountain to carry air for the jackhammers from the compressors below. In cold weather, a liquid gas was injected in a fine mist into the pipeline beyond the compressors to prevent

awe-inspiring and awesome…so glad we saw it!

HIGHLIGHTS
AND LOWLIGHTS

Seeing Mount Rushmore was definitely a highlight of epic proportions. Mostly because it was there, big, real and amazing. Cole and I sat and listened to this guy singing songs about America, and I remember feeling really thankful that I lived here. It was simply an idyllic setting to be patriotic.

When they lit up the mountain, we were all a little in awe because it goes from pitch black darkness, where you can't even make out the outline of the presidents, to this slow, gradual illumination that's pretty awesome. The lady on the PA said, "You won't be able to get the pictures with your cameras unless you have a really good camera." Well, I think I did pretty good, grain and all.

I'm so glad to have visited this historic site. I wouldn't be at all surprised if we pass by this way again in future years.

SCRAPBOOK INCOMPLETION SYNDROME

So, are you sick of this album yet? I will admit my biggest scrapbook weakness, but only to you: I have a really hard time finishing theme albums. There, I said it. There's no going back.

What happens is this: I get an idea, come up with a design, scrap like gangbusters for a day, then put it on the shelf to finish at another time. Then the weeks and months begin to fly by.

And you know what? It's okay. It really is. Because I made a **materials file** that contains the papers and other scrapbooking stuff I'll need to continue working on it later. A materials file serves as your central storage for all of the stuff that goes into making a simple scrapbook. It keeps everything you need for your scrapbook in one place so you don't waste time trying to find it all again. That way, you're ready to jump right back in without skipping a beat, whether it's the next day or six months later.

HOW TO SHARE THE STORY

If you really want to capture the details from your vacation, keep a travel log along the way. I brought along a cute Russell+Hazel notebook, and every night I'd write about what we did that day. It gave me a chance to record the meltdowns, the moments of magic, or simply a blow-by-blow account of the day. It was very useful when I finally sat down to make this album.

HOW'D YOU ACTUALLY MAKE IT?

To create all my pages, I used Adobe InDesign. I set up an 8½ x 11 landscape document and printed my pages full-bleed (all the way to the edge of the page) on my Hewlett Packard photo printer. That's how I was able to make the little boxes of color print right to the edge. I could've used squares of cardstock to achieve the same effect, but I really wanted the type color to match the boxes exactly.

BE FLEXIBLE

When I got to my Yellowstone photos, I realized I didn't have enough vertical shots to fill up the space completely. So I made a type strip to run along the bottom of the page, to fill the space. I used the same typeface and a reverse type technique (see p. 100).

ONE MORE THING

My camera battery lasted until we got to Yellowstone, where I had to break down and buy a (gasp!) disposable camera. Guess which shots were taken with the disposable? All but the opening shot. So much for high-end digital technology, right? It's the memories that count.

It is not down in any maps; true places never are.

HERMAN MELVILLE

days four & five

the coolest park in america

YELLOWSTONE

DAY FOUR
AUGUST 16, 2004

Today was a driving through the mountains day, and it was absolutely gorgeous.

We reached the East entrance to Yellowstone National Park at around 3:30 p.m., and drove through, taking all the sights we could in.

We stopped at Old Faithful briefly, but had just missed the eruption. We also stopped at a couple of the Geyser Pool areas to take a peek.

That's when my camera officially died. Que sera, sera.

We decided to come back into the park the next day. We were a bit tired, needing both dinner and a dip in a hotel pool, so we headed off to our hotel in West Yellowstone.

Chinese food for grown-ups. I can't remember what the kids had. More Olympics, and off to slumberland.

Suffice to say, the following day was amazing. Yellowstone has so much and I feel like we just barely saw it, really. Definitely down on the "list of places to revisit."

steaming geysers, bubbling paint pots, dead camera batteries...ahhhh

DAY FIVE
AUGUST 17, 2004

Yellowstone was amazing. I will admit, however, Old Faithful could have been more dramatic. Nevertheless, it was a cool, cool day a the park. We walked around geyser pools, bubbling paint pots and other undeniable examples of just how ever-changing this big old planet is. That's what is so cool—seeing the evidence of what are world is truly made up of.

Some of it was beautiful, and some of it, just plain smelly. There was one geyser pool in particular that was giving off a constant, thick cloud of steam. Aidan was not having any part of tooling around the little boardwalk that surrounded it. Finally, after much coaxing, she gave in, and walked through the warm, somewhat smelly steam.

I would love to go back there one day. There is really too much to take in properly in just a day and a half. We'll definitely return.

and we learned a valuable lesson...disposable cameras will do in a pinch!

the things he says

I live with a walking quote generator. His name is Coleman, and he's six years old. He says the most hilarious, charming and sometimes obscure things a parent could ever hope to hear. They come, rapid fire, throughout the course of any given day. Sometimes, I stop laughing long enough to write them down. Sometimes, I don't make it that far. But this is exactly the kind of stuff I want to be scrapbooking.

So I bought a small, spiral-bound mini-scrapbook to create one of my favorite albums called *The Things You Say*.

I created a couple of text boxes on my computer, using a reverse text technique (see p. 100). I typeset the quotes, print them out, and place them in the album, along with whatever recent, random photos I have of my little word wizard.

It's not comprehensive document of everything he says, but it does capture little pieces of how his amazing and unpredictable mind works.

This is the stuff that both he and I will lose over time if I don't record it. How much of what you said at six do you recall? This album will be the one we go back to often through the years. The one that will make him laugh. The one that will help him—and me—remember. The one he will read to his own six year old. The one that personifies just a tiny bit of who he was in 2005. This, to me, is what scrapbooking is all about.

"Allow myself,
to introduce...
myself."
AUSTIN POWERS

Coley, may the world know you
by what you say. And also be
highly entertained by it. CZ

Cole and I were driving in the
car, listening to "Steam" by Peter
Gabriel. There's a line in the song
that goes, "When I lose sight of
the track..." and Cole says, "MOM!
When Peter said 'track', I saw a
train track!" To which I replied,
half-listening "Oh." And he says,

**"MOM! That's
synchronicity!"**

JAN 1 9 2005

Cole was having trouble falling
asleep, and called me in. He said
he was thinking bad thoughts, so I
told him to think about Saints
games, and all of the Lego sets
he'd hope to one day own. He said
it wasn't working. "I wish I could
drain my head," he said. And I
told him to think about the things
he loved. When I asked him, "What
things do you love, Coley?" He
said, simply, "You."

JAN 2 2 2005

A WORK IN PROGRESS

Some albums are works in
progress. I've been slowly adding
entries to this one for nearly a year.
Most of the time, I just write down
his quote on a Post-it and stick it
on a blank page, to format and
print out when the mood strikes.
Once I'm ready to add the quote,
I try to give it some context: where
he was, and what circumstances
led up to what he said.

"I'm into disasters"
Cole, to his new babysitter,
while meeting her for
the first time.

Aidan was talking about how
scientists predict that one day,
years from now, there will likely
be another ice age, and Cole says,
**"Well, good thing we're
the ones with clothes!"**

JAN 2 2 2005

but what about holidays?

A lot of my scrapbooking completely bypasses the big events and celebrations of my life. I'm perfectly okay with this. However, I meet a lot of scrapbookers who can't fathom the idea of not scrapbooking every holiday or every birthday. Let me be the first to say: if this is what makes you happy, then by all means, do it!

With that in mind, I was looking over the lack of holiday pages in my scrapbook albums and decided to jump in, head first, and make a simple theme album about one holiday: Halloween.

A theme album is the perfect place to house your favorite holiday memories and photos. Plus, it provides a quick, simple way to show a chronological timeline of my kids over the years. One thing to notice: my pictures from the early years kind of suck. Why? Because I wasn't a scrapbooker in the early days, and I didn't take 176 pictures on Halloween like I do now. Good photos or not, I was still able to recall the details of each All Hallow's Eve with little trouble.

boo

a journey through the Zielske
halloween celebrations,
which we all know is simply a
clever ruse to get more candy

SO SIMPLE, IT'S SCARY

I love this little album. I started it in the fall of 2004 because I wanted to have a record of our Halloween celebrations throughout the years. I dug out old snapshots from each year, enlarged them using my scanner, and wrote the memories I could muster. This album contains a title page, opening quote, dedication, and filler pages. I keep the template for the page titles and journaling on my computer, so every Hallows Eve, it's ready to go when I am.

TITLE PAGE

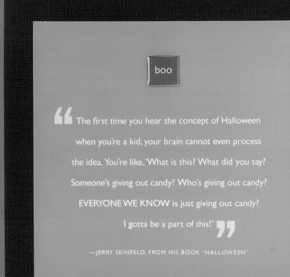

> " The first time you hear the concept of Halloween
> when you're a kid, your brain cannot even process
> the idea. You're like, 'What is this? What did you say?
> Someone's giving out candy? Who's giving out candy?
> EVERYONE WE KNOW is just giving out candy?
> I gotta be a part of this!' "
>
> —JERRY SEINFELD, FROM HIS BOOK "HALLOWEEN"

boo

a message from the

queen bee

Halloween 2004 is less than a week away, and while I was desperately
trying to find a new costume to wear this year, and perhaps retire the
infamous bee costume, I realized something valuable: being a bee is
my tradition. Changing your costume every year…well, that's just kid's
stuff. And that's exactly my point! It IS kid's stuff!

This is a little album of our ever-changing Halloween looks, for as
long as we get to create them. Halloween is fun, and magical, and cool.
And it's high-time I get busy remembering each and every one. Here's
to getting as much candy as humanly possible and remembering the
magic of becoming whatever you can dream up, or…whatever your
mom can afford to buy you in the Target costume aisle.

first halloween
the clown

Aidan's first Halloween. It was so dang exciting to dress you up and take pictures of you. Oh my GOSH! You were the cutest clown ever in the history of the world! We didn't take you out to trick or treat. I mean, you couldn't even walk yet. No, we just let you sit on a blanket in the family room and look adorable.

The hat didn't stay on too long. And I'm fairly certain your costume was soaked in drool after about 20 minutes. But there you were on your first Halloween. Our little trick or treat! Tell me honestly, has there ever been a more adorable clown? I think not.

seasoned pros
dorothy
AND the dalmation

In the year 2000, Aidan was obsessed with the Wizard of Oz. She watched it, she sang in, and when Halloween rolled around, she became it. Grandma Mac bought her the pricey get up, complete with ruby slippers, at F.A.O. Schwartz at the Mall of America. I vaguely recall some sort of ensuing meltdown, but it's all a bit fuzzy now.

I can't recall if Coley picked out his costume, or if it was an example of Mother Run Amock on the Target costume aisle. Whatever the case, they looked pretty dang cute.

HOW DO-ABLE IS THIS?

One year, two pictures, a little journaling. This is simple scrapbooking! I created a template for the journaling once, and for each entry, I just retype the title and journaling.

This is an album that will be fun for the kids to look at when they're all grown up and responsible, don't you think?

costumes that last
woody
AND the cheerleader

It's funny…but I remember very little of this year. I recall Coley didn't want to wear his costume, or go trick or treating. Aidan? She was raring to go, as she is every year. The weather was again unseasonably warm, allowing the kids to actually show off those fabulous costumes.

This was the year I started scrapbooking, and yet, I still didn't get the fact that you should take more than a few shots of your kids on Halloween. Sigh. One thing's for certain: they sure were cute!

2001

eBay finds
zorro
AND THE flower child

This was the year of the great eBay search for costumes. With Daddy's eBay savvy, Aidan was able to score a flower child/hippie chick kind of get-up, and Cole was trying in vain to get a Skeleton costume, with glow-in-the-dark bones.

Daddy got one, but when it arrived, it was a toddler size. So, he kept trying to win other auctions. In the meantime, Coley and Mom went to the Halloween Spirit store and picked up Zorro for good measure. Cole kept telling people he was going as "Zorcon." In the end, the kids got a major haul, didn't freeze and didn't even get sick tummies. Oh, and yes, Mom was a bee for the 17th year in a row.

2004

the coolest album ever

The coolest albums I have ever made are ones I'm still making, and I got the ideas straight from scrapbook genius Stacy Julian, founder of *Simple Scrapbooks* magazine, author and motivational speaker extraordinaire. Thanks to her, my kids will have school albums they'll enjoy forever, and making them won't send their mother to a Scrapbook Rehab Center for the Perpetually Stressed and Behind.

I'm talking about the *School of Life* album concept, first introduced in Stacy's book, *Simple Scrapbooks*. Each year of school is summarized in two simple spreads. An entire grade school career can fit into a single album. You simply design a look and feel, gather photos and any other materials you'll need (storing them in a materials file) and at the end of each school year, sit down and make your pages. Done!

TITLE PAGE

HAPPINESS

This album makes me happy. Why? Because when it's done, it will be a quick, chronological snapshot of Aidan. And because I really don't approach scrapbooking chronologically, I feel like it's a nice "alternative" to what I usually do, and will satisfy any need Aidan may feel in the future to have a visual record of her school years.

third grade

Ms. Green's Class

Crossroads Elementary, St. Paul, Minnesota

2004/2005

Age Eight

1 You and Isa at the end of the year Crossroads picnic.

2 Your 9th birthday party sleepover, with Isa, Melody, Nicollette and Cara.

1 You and Ms. Green at the Peace Site dedication.

3 You and Isa, at the Peace Site dedication.

school stuff

1 Your official class picture.

2 Your Australia report: the report that crushed all the other children, and was done very late at night, with a little help from Mom and Dad.

3 Your softball picture.

DOUBLE DUTY PHOTOS

Two of the three photos in this album show up on other layouts

in this book. And that's okay! This album is for Aidan to take

with her when she one day flies away.

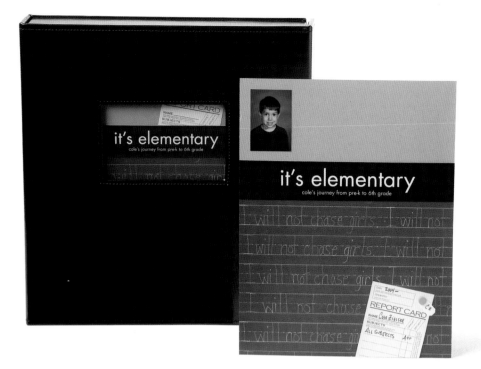

Four pages for each year of school. Now you may be thinking, "But there are so many more shots that need to go in there," and you may be having trouble breathing, but listen to me: I believe my kids are going to think this is the coolest quick snapshot of their school years ever. And these are the only albums they will be allowed to take with them when they move out!

I believe that scrapbooking should be simple. I know a lot of women want to document their kid's school lives, and this approach is an easy, guilt-free way to do just that.

Extra photos from the school year will go into a family photo album.

CREATING A MATERIALS FILE

Cole is just getting started on his academic journey, so when I came up with the basic design for his album, I picked up at least a dozen of the 7Gypsies report cards, and about 30 sheets of the Rusty Pickle patterned paper. I keep them together in a plastic paper keeper, so when I'm ready to work on his Kindergarten section, which I'll do at the end of the school year, everything I need to create the pages is right there.

For both kids' albums, I have templates on my computer for the page titles and, in Aidan's case, the journaling entries. I decided not to journal on Cole's yet. I may go back and add some thoughts, but then again, I might not.

pre-kindergarten

school stuff

going back to high school

High school. Two words that can send shivers down the spine of any well-adjusted adult. If high school evokes memories of the best time of your life, you and I didn't go to the same school!

And yet, I had photos. Lots of them. Tucked away inside an old foot locker was this album full of photos in decidedly non-acid-free magnetic pages, just beckoning to come out and find a new life. So out they came...

With adhesive remover in hand, I spent a weekend removing all of the photos and putting them in piles: friends, snapshots, dances. While doing this, I came up with a simple framework for the album. I'd focus on my best friends from high school, giving each girl her own section spread, and the rest of the album would include a dedication and simple filler pages of all the random photos. The journaling would be heavy in the front, and non-existent in the latter part of the album.

highschool

days

Bad hair, horrid fashions and few dates,
but friends that lasted a lifetime
A place I can't say I'd like to go back to,
but a place to remember all the same.

Cascade High School 1981–1984

friend

you couldn't pay me enough

to go back there. Sorry. It's the one place in my life I am so thankful I never have to visit again. High school was simply a means to an end—an education to prepare me for the rest of life. Now I don't want to sound overly bitter, but high school was kind of a pain in the ass. Why? Because let's face it—to be yourself was social suicide. No one wanted originality. They simply wanted to fit in. And I was the biggest fitter-inner of them all! That is how you survive in high school.

I guess the memories would have been better were it not for one glaring event that stands out: when I got my hair cut short towards the end of my senior year, people freaked out on me. It was the last straw in what I'd always subconsciously knew was a giant social ruse. That's when I knew that getting out of high school was a one-way ticket to personal freedom and the only way I was ever going to get to be me.

So...if all the bitterness, why the scrapbook? Well there were a few things that made high school worth it. Molly, Shaun, Sharon—and later—Kathy and Carolyn. Those are the people who, when I remember the nutty, youthful, insane, mundane and silly stuff we did, make me smile. I have photos. I have memories. The good stuff is always about the people. Always.

TRUTH OR DARE?

I'm really not as bitter as I sound in the journaling. Really. But whenever possible, I like to be honest with my scrapbooking. That is my biggest motivator, being truthful in the stories I share. And you know what? High school was not a bed of roses. Let's just say I took the good stuff with me: my friends and my sanity.

you couldn't pay me enough

to go back there. Sorry. It's the one place in my life I am so thankful I never have to visit again. High school was simply a means to an end—an education to prepare me for the rest of life. Now I don't want to sound overly bitter, but high school was kind of a pain in the ass. Why? Because let's face it—to be yourself was social suicide. No one wanted originality. They simply wanted to fit in. And I was the biggest fitter-inner of them all! That is how you survive in high school.

I guess the memories would have been better were it not for one glaring event that stands out: when I got my hair cut short towards the end of my senior year, people freaked out on me. It was the last straw in what I'd always subconsciously knew was a giant social ruse. That's when I knew that getting out of high school was a one-way ticket to personal freedom and the only way I was ever going to get to be me.

So...if all the bitterness, why the scrapbook? Well there were a few things that made high school worth it. Molly, Shaun, Sharon—and later—Kathy and Carolyn. Those are the people who, when I remember the nutty, youthful, insane, mundane and silly stuff we did, make me smile. I have photos. I have memories. The good stuff is always about the people. Always.

I picked one of my favorite color schemes—hot pink and chartreuse—to use with these old, blurry photos. Plus, I wanted to prove to myself that you can make practically any photos work with any color scheme. And you know what? It worked. This album makes me happy, bad perm and all.

I followed a simple design scheme for this album. I have yet to create the entries for my other two girlfriends. So Shaun and Sharon, if you're reading this, you'll be in there soon. I promise.

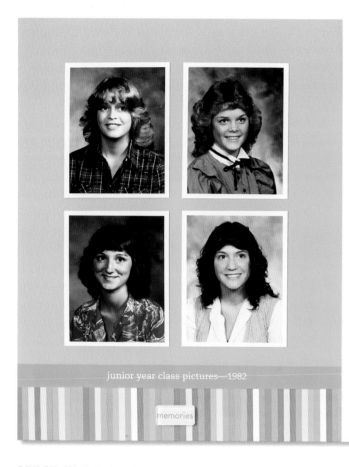

junior year class pictures—1982

memories

 the core four

Molly, Shaun, Sharon and Cathy. That was the core high school four. I know how I came to know Molly and Shaun—the fabulous Everett Rollerfair Skatedeck. I can't quite recall how Sharon came into the mix. But there we were, a united front on our first day at Cascade High School in 1981.

People came and went, but essentially, the four of us formed our own little high school clique. We moved in and out of other circles with ease—the preppies or the stoners—which is funny to me now that really, there weren't that many groups you could belong to back then. I suppose you could break it down further, but this will serve the purpose at hand.

And so, it was just us. During most of those years, Molly was with Jeff, Sharon was with Rick, and Shaun was with so many different people I couldn't recount them if I tried. Me? One or two romantic trysts was all I managed to wrangle out of my high school years. More on that later. It seemed that boys just liked to tell me their problems because I was so easy to talk to.

I remember thinking I was destined to become a psychiatrist in my later years, because I was a good listener and offered such valuable advice. As if a 16-year-old had all the answers! Ah, those were the days.

STUCK IN A TIME WARP?

Do you have crappy photos from the 80s, 70s or earlier? However bad the shots may be, they are still attached to memories. Use them. Also, work with colors that make you happy. You don't have to use colors that are associated with a specific period of time. Although the pink on this album is kind of late 80s, don't you think?

A LITTLE SCANNER FUN

I scanned a bunch of my high school shots to make photo strips (see top spread on facing page) in Photoshop. Photo strips just remind me of high school. Let's hear it for digital imaging!

molly christina moran

through thick and thin

One person made high school worthwhile: Molly. What can I say that I haven't already said about Molly Moran? Because now suddenly, I'm at a loss for words...okay, not really!

I remember walking down the hallways of Cascade High School with Molly and being so proud that she was my best friend. I always felt like she had an air of, not necessarily mysteri-ousness, but an air of untouchable-ness. And, by association, I would have that too. I just thought she was cool, and couldn't quite figure out why she liked me so much. Go figure.

Lord knows we had ups and downs, going back into the eighth grade when I made the erroneous decision to "go out" with Jeff for a week or two. Ah yes...but we always came back together. Me and Molly, that is.

Molly made high school fun and bearable. I'm so glad after all these years, she's still there, ready to listen, ready to laugh, and ready to celebrate that our high school friendship turned out to be the most enduring one of all.

those fabulous dances

everything counts

I scrapbook about a lot of stuff. And even though I try really hard to focus on the tiny details of my life, sometimes the basic things get overlooked. Thus, the impetus for my *Every Little Thing* album. It all started with paper towels. Yes. Paper towels are the inspiration behind this album.

It's also my friend Donna Downey's fault. After working on the design of Donna's *Yes, It's a Scrapbook* series, I was inspired to try something I wouldn't normally do, like cover chipboard with patterned paper and make an album bound together with leather ties. My goals were clear: one, make a funky, Donna-styled album; and two, use it to pay tribute to paper towels, french fries, e-mail, and other random little things that make my life a nicer place to be.

The resulting album sits in a place of honor on my piano, on a little easel. And if people come over, they can remark on how weird it is that I'm so taken with paper towels. But it is cute, no?

TITLE PAGE

I know what the **BIG** things are…

family *faith*
love HEALTH
hope

… and I try, every day,
to never take for granted the big things in life.

But what about the little things?

This is an album to celebrate the things that aren't so big, that aren't so obvious. The little things that add so much to my life, that bring me peace and joy, and that I also never want to take for granted. From clean sheets to discovering there is just enough cinnamon sugar for one more piece of toast. They might not be as flashy, but they're every bit as vital in the entire scheme of this thing called "my life."

Here's to remembering every little thing.

SHOULD OR COULD?

What are the little things in your life that you want to acknowledge? Do summer pedicures make you happy? How about microwave ovens? What about fresh-from-the-deep-fryer McDonald's fries? These are just a few of the "little" things I scrapbooked in this album.

*paper*towels

*every*little*thing*

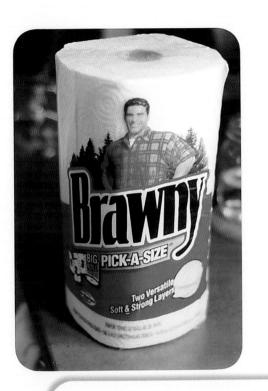

THINK ABOUT IT

Is writing about paper towels a waste of time? Possibly. But I'd argue that if you acknowledge the things that make your life easier and happier, however small and insignificant, you realize that happiness isn't always about the big things in life. It can give you a greater appreciation for the little stuff.

How did the *pioneers* do it?

I was thinking about this alot on our family vacation, as we're flying down the highway at 80 miles per hour. I often think what a horrible pioneer I would have made. Heat, wagon trains, consumption…and if that wasn't bad enough—those pioneer women didn't have paper towels!

I love paper towels. Paper towels tell me that everything is right in the universe. Paper towels tell me I am a good and capable mother. Paper towels mean I don't actually touch toast crusts, or potato peelings or anything else that will get my hands all sticky and in need of a quick washing. Paper towels are something that, when they get dirty, you throw them away.

Dan, who is my tree-huggin', waste-not, want-not hunk of man, didn't grow up with paper towels, and I don't think he appreciates or understands this deep connection I feel with the Brawny man. I just tell him, "Paper towels remind me of my Mom." That usually clears me to buy another roll.

I prefer Pick-a-Size rolls, but really, anything will do in a pinch. The only time paper towels cause me the least bit of concern is when the roll is nearly gone and I realize there is no back-up tucked beneath the sink. Then, I treat those last few sheets as if they were rolled up 20-dollar bills.

It's a little thing really, paper towels. A little thing that I love. Oh sure, I do have roughly 15 white dish towels, and yes, they do get used. But they don't quite measure up to the most amazing, all-purpose invention that trees ever gave us. Better go check how much is left on the roll.

I wanna be like Oprah

It's true. I do. But there are a few obstacles. Well, okay, more like billions of them. But that doesn't stop my admiration, nor the inspiration I've gotten from watching 20 years of her show. (Yes, I did watch when I was 19. Am I really that old?)

Years ago, Oprah suggested people keep gratitude journals. This was before I was a scrapbooker, but you better believe, if Oprah was telling me to do something, I was taking action. It was such an exercise in helping me to see, with crystal clarity, that people and experience were the things I was truly grateful for. Every day, my list was the same. It was all about love and experience. No material item ever made that list.

So fast forward several years. Oprah writes her "What I know for sure" column in each issue of O magazine. I finally sat down and made a simple album—my own take on the same concept. 100 percent me...except for the title, which I borrowed from an Oprah book club selection a few years back. I really should get a "What Would Oprah Do?" bracelet, huh?

WHAT DO YOU KNOW?

Can you answer that question? If you can, you've got a simple theme album halfway completed. Share your beliefs, your convictions, the things you've learned on your journey through life. This is the stuff that matters. This is the opportunity to tell it like it is. Break it up into sections. My album has four: love, friendship, creativity and life. I just sat and wrote from the gut. I know when I open this album in 30 years, if I'm still around and kicking, these things will ring as true then as they do today.

this much i know is true

this much i know is true

There are things I know. Things in my heart that I believe are true. Things that I would argue until my last breath. Some are things that matter. Some are slightly less critical. All have one thing in common: I believe them to be the truth. And so, in this world of ours that is often less than crystal clear, this much I know is true.

about love

I KNOW THAT I HAVE ALWAYS BEEN LOVED. IT'S SOMETHING I'VE ALWAYS KNOWN & FELT DEEPLY. I KNOW THAT I CHOSE A PARTNER WHO LOVES ME UNCONDITIONALLY. I KNOW THAT WE ARE TOGETHER FOR THE LONG HAUL. I KNOW THAT LOVE IS ALSO ABOUT RESPECT. THAT THE TWO GO HAND IN HAND. I KNOW THAT HAVING CHILDREN HAS COMPLETELY REDEFINED WHAT LOVE REALLY IS. IT'S PUSHED THE SCALE OFF THE CHARTS. I KNOW THAT IN THE END, IF YOU STRIP IT ALL AWAY, THE LOVE OF FAMILY AND FRIENDS IS REALLY THE ONLY THING THAT WILL EVER MATTER. WHICH GOES BACK TO KNOWING I'VE ALWAYS BEEN LOVED, AND THAT I NEED TO BE SURE THAT THOSE IN MY LIFE, WILL ALWAYS KNOW THE SAME.

MIX AND MATCH
While I created my titles and photo collages on the computer, I wanted this album to have a bit more of a personal touch. Thus the handwritten journaling. It's absolutely okay to mix handwriting and computer fonts.

everyone's doing it

I can't actually back that up, but I do know that everyone could be doing it: making a *Photos I Love* theme album. Another conceptual gem, courtesy of my friend Stacy Julian, this album has become an annual staple on my scrapbook project to-do list. It's a fun, relaxing way to scrapbook those photos that you absolutely adore. The ones that make you smile every time you see them.

Now, here are the rules. Are you ready? Because you might miss them: none! That's right, it's a lawless scrapland. Anything goes! You just find your favorite photos, write a note about the photo, put a date on it, and scrap it any way, and in any format you please.

I tend to use 8 x 8 albums for mine, and my only rule is that I convert all my favorite shots to black and white. Why? Because if you haven't picked it up by now, I like black and white photos. Then, I can pick some funky patterned papers and go to town.

IS THAT LEGAL?

After I made my title for the front window of the album, I realized I didn't have another "f" to repeat it on the title page. So, I called it something different on the inside. And yes, I am aware that the phrase, "The best and most fave of" is a little bit like caveman speak, but it gets the point across, right? I'm trying to be less hung up on getting it perfect. And you know what? I think it's working. And I'm having way more fun scrapbooking because of it.

TITLE PAGE

MATCHING SHOES | MARCH 2005

It reminds me of how much fun I get to have hanging out with Donna and Ali. How, even though the stress of those CKUs sometimes kills me, getting to connect with people I like so much is a good thing. And it makes me remember how proud they were that I went out of my box and bought pink matching shoes.

GRANDPA AND COLE | MAY 2005

The look on Cole's face. The intense concentration of my Dad to get that flying thing up and in the air. Every time I see this shot I smile. It feels like the quintessential grandpa and grandson shot. I truly cherish any photos of the kids with my mom and dad, because we don't see them nearly enough.

COLE AND CHICKEN | JUNE 2005

Even though I already scrapped this photo, there's a reason: I adore it. It looks like total crap, color wise, but the expression on his face. Could the kid be any more proud that he wrangled a chicken? Wouldn't you feel exactly the same way if you'd managed to chase that thing down? Me? Definitely.

KIDS IN MUD | JULY 2005

They just don't care that they are sitting in a filthy, stinky mud puddle in the middle of our street. I shot a ton of photos of this slice of life. One I scrapbooked. Most I didn't. But this one definitely makes me smile every time I see it. And remembering how we hosed them all down in the backyard before coming in the house. Now that was funny.

A YEAR OF FAVORITES

I organize my photos using iPhoto software for the Mac. And each time I come across a picture that makes me smile, or gasp, or laugh, I put it into a folder called "Favorites." Then, at the end of the year, I make black and white enlargements of all those pictures, write a few words about them, and put them in my album. This album truly celebrates one of the things that make scrapbooking so fun—photos I love!

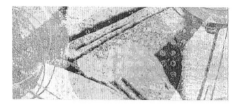

Is for Aidan, and authentic, and amazing, and adventurous, and agreeable at times, and many other lovely "a" words. But since when did it also stand for Audrey—as in Audrey Hepburn? It is just me? Or does this photo to the right look like an ad for a remake of *Breakfast at Tiffany's*? It's gotta be the expression. It's just so 1960-effervescent-I'm-an-A-list-starlet. And it's just so you. December '05

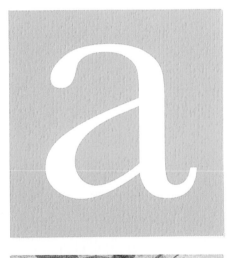

enjoy

In the end, we scrapbook because it makes us happy. We find our

groove. We develop our style. We find unique approaches. We

organize. We play. We become more aware of the world around us.

And ultimately, we nurture the spirit of our personal creativity.

At the core of it all is the simple joy of playing with paper, telling

a story, and making stuff that's really, really cool.

finding your groove

Fall 2001. Cathy starts scrapbooking. She makes the layout you see on the facing page. The love affair begins. But what to do next?

Good question. For me, the answer was buying scrapbooking magazines and idea books. If I was going to do this hobby, I had to familiarize myself with the paradigms of working with paper, photos and adhesives. And why? Because you have to know the basics before you can move onto adapting and interpreting the process, and eventually, discovering your own style.

The first book I bought was *Scrapbooking Secrets* by Becky Higgins. Becky has helped many a scrapbooker find ways to make pictures and paper look good together. I think I tried every technique in that book. The layout below is essentially a lift of various elements from Becky's book.

The other key thing I learned from Becky was that clean lines, meaningful stories, and simple design were perfectly okay and would never go out of style. I didn't have to buy a heat embosser to be a successful scrapbooker. I just had to continue adapting what I saw until things started to click.

YOU LIFT, YOU LEARN

The layout below, circa 2001, is another example of me trying to find my groove as a scrapbooker. You gotta admit, those torn hearts are pretty cute! (Thanks goes to Becky Higgins, of course, for the inspiration. To this day, I couldn't come up with something that clever!)

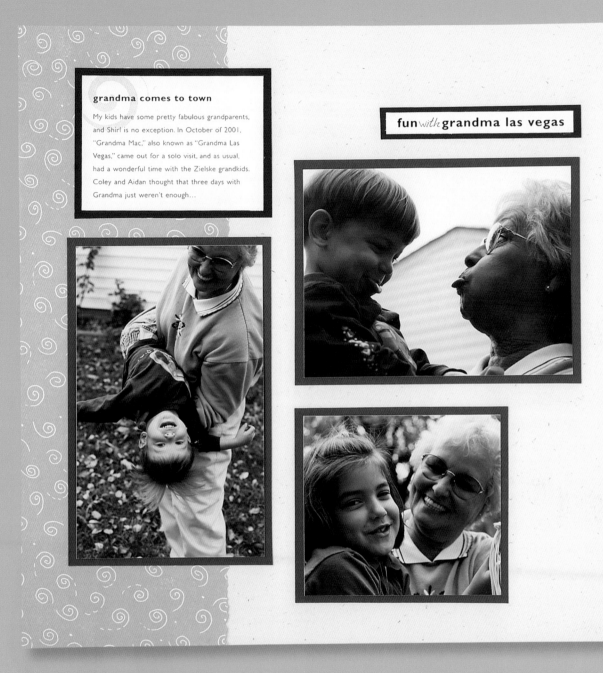

grandma comes to town

My kids have some pretty fabulous grandparents, and Shirl is no exception. In October of 2001, "Grandma Mac," also known as "Grandma Las Vegas," came out for a solo visit, and as usual, had a wonderful time with the Zielske grandkids. Coley and Aidan thought that three days with Grandma just weren't enough…

fun *with* grandma las vegas

WHERE IT ALL BEGAN

This is the first scrapbook layout I ever did. It was the fall of 2001. I was so ecstatic when this thing was finished. Yes…I scrapped black and white photos from the start. Yes…I used equal margin spacing. Yes…I used type on my page. No…there weren't a lot of embellishments. What's funny to me is how little my style has changed. Oh sure, I got a little funkier after this layout, but eventually, I settled in and found my groove. And by trusting your own instincts, so will you.

LISTEN FOR THE CLICK

The "click" is when you begin to identify what is working for you as a scrapbooker. The "click" is the birth of your personal style. For me, the layout you see on this page, previously published in the *Creating Keepsakes Hall of Fame* book, was my bona fide click. It's when I realized what I wanted to do with scrapbooking: tell good stories, add a photo and keep it simple.

I realized I wanted to scrap in 8½ x 11. And I wanted to use fonts. And I wanted to use minimal photos. This was what felt most comfortable to me, and I began to embrace my style.

My style involves several things, and I'm guessing it's not too hard to figure out what those things are. Here's the run-down of what my pages usually consist of:

- black and white photos—one to three of them
- occasional enlargements
- color-blocked designs
- equal margin spacing
- computer fonts (a few favorites used time and again)
- paper flowers and brads
- rub-on alphabets
- quippy titles
- elements that run all the way to the edge
- a smattering of patterned paper
- lots of journaling

These are the working parameters of my personal style. As I was working on layouts for this book, I kept thinking, "I should really try to break out and do something different. Everything I do looks the same! I wonder if people will notice?"

And you know what? I hope you did notice. Because that is me being comfortable within the boundaries of my own style. Just as I'm hopelessly attached to my old orange sweatshirt (see page at right), I'm equally attached to the style in which I scrapbook. It makes me happy and it feels like me.

Never one to hold back your thoughts and feelings on any given subject, you recently expressed your dismay at the lack of color photographs I had been taking. Everytime I would bring a roll home from processing, and you would see it was yet another round of black and whites, you'd tell me: "Mom, I will not let you take any more pictures of me unless they are in color." And while you are an artistic girl, it seems you have yet to develop an appreciation for the sheer simplicity and timelessness of the black and white photo. For that, I forgive you. You are, afterall and unbelievably, five.

When this photo was taken, I was borrowing a friend's camera to get the tight, close-up shots I'm never able to get with my own, and you told me:

Mom, there had better be color film in there!

And this was your expression when I confirmed your worst expectations. This is you, Aidan. One of the many faces you show. And it's both priceless and dead on.

Your spirit is so strong and so full of confidence. You say what you mean and you mean what you say. In so many ways we are different. And so very, very many, we are alike. We may butt heads at times, but how I admire your strength. How I pray it remains with you, and grows...

comfortable.

dependable.

always cozy.

stretched out.

marginally stained.

it just feels like me.

the infamous orange sweatshirt, circa 2005

PERFORM A STYLE AUDIT

So what's your "orange sweatshirt"? What elements make you happy and comfortable? Sit down and thumb through your layouts. Identify the approaches, techniques and types of embellishments that you use on a regular basis. Pull out a piece of paper—or better yet—make a scrapbook page about your scrapbooking style. Celebrate the stuff that makes your pages unique and also makes them "you."

create a style file

If the world around us is truly rife with ideas for the picking, then we as scrapbookers need to start harnessing those little bits of inspiration for use on our scrapbook pages. Maybe you see an ad with a color scheme you'd never thought to use before. Maybe you see a photograph and think, "I'd like to try taking a shot like that."

Whatever the case, if you find something that speaks to you, save it in your style file. I use a binder from Russell+Hazel along with a small lunch pail from BasicGrey to store all the little tidbits that speak to me artistically. It's not hard once you start looking for ideas. For example, I end up tearing at least ten or more pages out of every issue of *Real Simple* magazine for my file. Whether it's a fresh color combo or a nice page layout, I keep them in one central location to pull out and revisit, especially when I'm in need of scrapbook design inspiration.

START COLLECTING IDEAS TODAY

Part of developing your style is to be aware of what appeals to you. Colors, designs, textures, ideas—all of these elements can provide inspiration for scrapbook layouts. So get busy. Make a binder or a style file that makes you happy, and fill it up.

I have no problem with all the gray hairs on my head

40

I really don't. But what is up with the wrinkles on the forehead? It looks like I'm constantly worried. And you know what? I'm just not. I will be 40 in three months. It doesn't feel weird to me at all. I'm ready. If 40 feels like you're comfortable in your own skin, at peace with much in the world, and thankful to be alive, then I'm already there. Now, where's that wrinkle cream?

MAGAZINES: THE NEW IDEA BOOKS!

When I saw the ad to the left, I thought, "Hey, that could be a cool scrapbook page." And when I realized the underlying "fake" ad was for wrinkle cream, it made me think, "Hey, I have wrinkles!" Combine that with the fact that I'm turning 40 this year, and you have not only a layout inspired by an ad design, but by the ad content as well.

scraplift the world at large

Once you've got your style file up and running, the fun begins. What is out there in the world that can inspire your scrapbooking? When you start to pay attention to color, shape and design, you realize that the Home Decor aisle at Target has a textile pattern you simply must lift now for your next page.

It's all about cultivating your creativity. And it doesn't mean going off the deep end artistically. Look at me! My pages are fairly stripped down and simple. Yes, my type usage is a bit more involved, but at the core, I make very simple pages. That doesn't stop me from being inspired by what I see around me.

Live life with your creative radar turned on. Even laundry can yield something other than heavy sighs and resignation if you're inspired to do a layout by the Bounce packaging colors.

Carry a small notebook with you in your handbag, too. Sometimes, in the strangest places, you might see something you'll want to remember. Keeping an eye on the surrounding world can supply you with an endless stream of ideas for scrapbooking. I'm not saying books like the one you're reading right now aren't helpful, but they don't even begin to scratch the potential of ideas that exist beyond the printed page. Go ahead—scraplift the world at large. It's waiting.

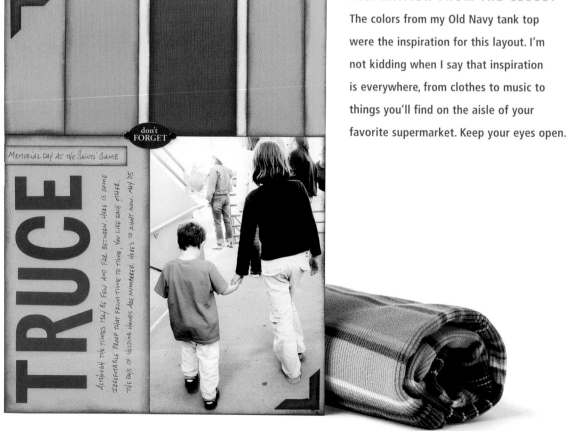

INSPIRATION FROM THE CLOSET

The colors from my Old Navy tank top were the inspiration for this layout. I'm not kidding when I say that inspiration is everywhere, from clothes to music to things you'll find on the aisle of your favorite supermarket. Keep your eyes open.

my name *Cathy Zielske*

childhood ambition *To Become a Writer*

fondest memory *One of them... Dan at the Airport in 1990.*

soundtrack *Green Day & Foo Fighters*

retreat *My House, when it's empty, quiet & clean*

wildest dream *To Meet Oprah*

proudest moment *Giving Birth to Aidan... Never knew i could do that!*

biggest challenge *Being Patient. Always.*

alarm clock *6:30 - 7 a.m., By my own internal clock*

perfect day *Any day at home, with family, & a possible nap.*

first job *Snack Bar Girl at the Rollerfair Skatedeck*

indulgence *Technology. Absolutely.*

last purchase *Scrapbook stuff... no surprise there.*

favorite movie *The Shawshank Redemption.*

inspiration *Everything. Pretty much Everything.*

NOV 20 2005

YOURS FOR THE TAKING

The world of print—magazines, newspapers and books—is a giant cornucopia of potential ideas for scrapbookers. I'm constantly inspired by what I see on the printed page. This layout above is a scraplift of an American Express ad. Not only that, it's another layout idea that you can use for a page about yourself!

It is a fun idea, similar to the list of questions I answered back on page 31. However computer illiterate you may think you are, this is simply a list with some lines drawn. No fancy footwork required. Another example of an idea culled from the world of print.

see box...step outside

Another way to boost your creativity is to step outside of your comfort zone every now and then. This might mean going to a museum and viewing an exhibit of fine art. Or, it could mean deciding to go a day with no hair product usage. Or, it could mean joining an online art journal class.

Because I would never choose to live a day without hair product, I opted for an online art journal class, taught by Shimelle Laine, an American artist/scrapbooker living in England. I was so excited to start I could barely contain myself. Each week, she would send e-mails with that particular week's assignment. Initially, I had a great time with the assignments, even though I will be the first to admit I wasn't bound to win any design awards.

It was a complete and total challenge, and truth be told, I fell way behind in the class. But what I realized by stepping outside of my safe little world was this: I am completely comfortable approaching the artistic side of my hobby the way I do. I don't have to hop on any new trend bandwagons. I can just be me.

That said, the value in trying other things—whatever they may be—can also give you tiny epiphanies over what works for you creatively and what doesn't. And it might just make you appreciate your own style and approach that much more.

TRY SOMETHING NEW

Sign up for a bookbinding course, or a pottery course, or a photography course, or any other course that will take you, temporarily, out of your comfort zone. In the end, you'll likely feel a renewed inspiration for the art you create every day with scrapbooking.

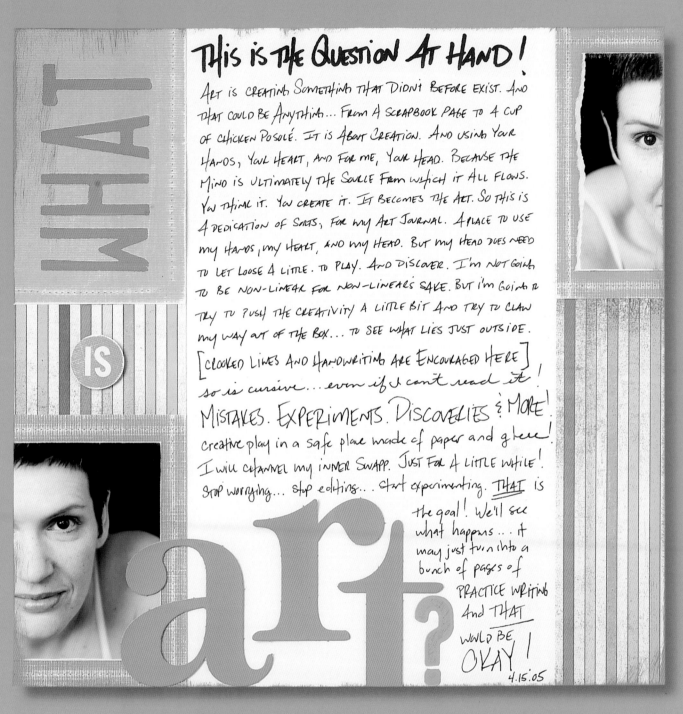

WHAT IS art?

THIS IS THE QUESTION AT HAND!

ART IS CREATING SOMETHING THAT DIDN'T BEFORE EXIST. AND THAT COULD BE ANYTHING... FROM A SCRAPBOOK PAGE TO A CUP OF CHICKEN POSOLÉ. IT IS ABOUT CREATION. AND USING YOUR HANDS, YOUR HEART, AND FOR ME, YOUR HEAD. BECAUSE THE MIND IS ULTIMATELY THE SOURCE FROM WHICH IT ALL FLOWS. YOU THINK IT. YOU CREATE IT. IT BECOMES THE ART. SO THIS IS A DEDICATION OF SORTS, FOR MY ART JOURNAL. A PLACE TO USE MY HANDS, MY HEART, AND MY HEAD. BUT MY HEAD DOES NEED TO LET LOOSE A LITTLE. TO PLAY. AND DISCOVER. I'M NOT GOING TO BE NON-LINEAR FOR NON-LINEAR'S SAKE. BUT I'M GOING TO TRY TO PUSH THE CREATIVITY A LITTLE BIT AND TRY TO CLAW MY WAY OUT OF THE BOX... TO SEE WHAT LIES JUST OUTSIDE.

[CROOKED LINES AND HANDWRITING ARE ENCOURAGED HERE] so is cursive... even if I can't read it!

MISTAKES. EXPERIMENTS. DISCOVERIES & MORE! creative play in a safe place made of paper and glue! I will channel my INNER SWAPP. JUST FOR A LITTLE WHILE! stop worrying... stop editing... start experimenting. THAT is the goal! We'll see what happens... it may just turn into a bunch of pages of PRACTICE WRITING And THAT WOULD BE OKAY!

4.15.05

ROOM TO PLAY

Every now and then it feels really good to do something I would never normally do. Initially, using my own handwriting was pushing the envelope in a major way. Now, I try to play with my scrapbook stuff a little more often to see what might happen.

I'm not going to leave behind the real me—linear, safe and predictable—for a complete foray into paper arts, but I believe there's value in trying something new. It opens my eyes to the possibilities of creative expression. Go out on a limb every now and then. I can guarantee you it will make your tree stronger.

organized...who, me?

Organization can be one of two things to any scrapbooker: a saving grace, or the bane of one's existence. I fall somewhere in between in the following organizational areas.

PHOTOS

I've been completely digital for almost two years now. While my boxes and piles of photos are much less obtrusive, my computer's hard drive is quickly filling up with thousands of digital files.

But I've tried to stick to a monthly regimen of photo printing and archiving. I use iPhoto (an Apple program) to organize all of my digital photos. I make a folder each month and create settings that place each "roll" I shoot into the appropriate month by date taken. Then, at the end of the month, I create a file of photos to

DEVELOP A SYSTEM

It's important for digital photographers to develop a system that works for them. It's also critical to back up your photos periodically. Nothing says "sad scrapbooker" like a catastrophic data loss.

print, make any necessary adjustments, and upload them to Shutterfly.com to get prints made.

Then, I back up that month's photos onto an external hard drive I use specifically for photo and other data backups. Further, I make photo CD backups that I keep in a binder. I'm hoping the day won't come when a catastrophic power surge blazes through my computer, but if it does, I'm fairly certain I would have a safely archived visual record of my life.

SUPPLIES

I'm not sure if this one is a saving grace, but it's definitely the area where I've got the upper hand. I've got a dedicated space in which to scrap (yes, it happens to be my dining room), and I've got designated spaces for my tools and supplies. It really helps my process. When I need to know where something is, I know exactly where to find it.

I organize my cardstock by color and my patterned paper by manufacturer. Everything else gets sorted accordingly. I refinished an old library card file to store embellishments. Rub-on alphabets in one drawer. Brads in another. Stickers in another. It's not perfect by any means, but it works for me. And until I win the lottery and have a scrapbooking wing added to my home, this will most definitely suffice.

I believe you can take any space—however spacious or small—and make it work for you.

SCRAPBOOK ALBUMS

And finally, my scrapbook album system. I use the term "system" loosely. I went from no system at all to one that, so far, is serving me pretty well. Here is how I organize my scrapbook pages. I should note that I use three-ring binder scrapbooks for almost all of my albums. I like how easy it is to add or rearrange pages. Plus, companies like Kolo, Pulp Paper Products and American Crafts are making the coolest binders you've ever seen!

PEOPLE

Each family member has their own 8½ x 11 binder. If a page is created about that person, it goes into his or her album. When that album is full, a new one is started. That's it. It's not determined by a calendar year, but rather, when it's full. Currently, the kids have four binders each. Dan has one, and I have one completed and one in progress.

FAMILY

Any layout that features more than one of us goes into the *Family* binder. This also includes pages about extended family. I currently have one completed binder and one in progress.

FRIENDS

Any page about friends goes here. This includes friends of my children as well. This is the place I document the friendships that enrich my life and the lives of my family. I have one completed *Friends* binder and one in progress.

CHRISTMAS

Any page about Christmas goes here. This binder only has about seven layouts, covering the past five years that I've been a scrapbooker. I'm just not a big holiday scrapbooker, but I needed to designate a binder for this purpose anyway. And it is red, so that makes sense, right?

12 X 12 PAGES

Because I've started making 12 x 12 pages, this is my current area that is a bit mixed up. I keep all of my 12 x 12 pages, regardless of the subject, in a large three-ring binder from American Crafts. However, I'm planning to break them up exactly the way I do my 8½ x 11 pages when the time comes. It just makes sense to me.

And that is it! If that qualifies as a system, then so be it. I like knowing that when I finish a page, it has a place to go. Almost anything else I scrapbook goes into a single-subject theme album, some of which I've shared with you in Chapter Four. And for those album formats, the size and shape are determined by the subject of the album.

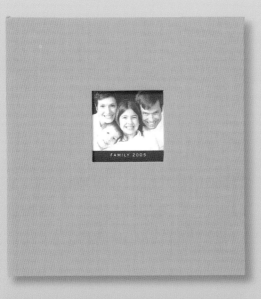

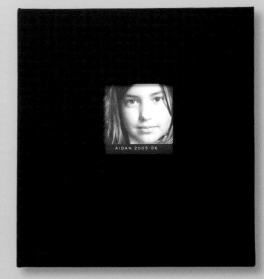

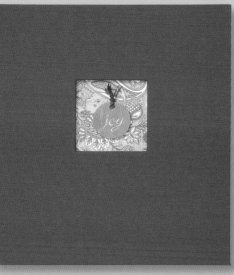

I'M A THREE-RING KIND OF GAL

Binders are my favorite scrapbook albums. They're easy to use, and come in beautiful colors. The albums on this page are all by Kolo. I like that I can easily take pages out or rearrange them. For my binders with windows, I usually print the name of the album on white cardstock, along with a photo appropriate for that particular album. Because I'm not a huge embellisher, this is how I add a touch of customization in a simple way.

what I've been trying to say

It all boils down to this: scrapbooking is cool. I'm not sure of any other way to say it. And that makes you cool by association for doing it, or even just thinking about it. Yes...you, me, and anyone else taking the time to combine memory with paper and glue. It's one giant club of cool.

It's "cool" because it's people taking the time to embrace their lives and to express creatively the stuff that matters and the stuff to remember. The real stuff of life.

And here's another cool thing: you don't have to scrapbook like me. That's the beauty of this hobby. There is room for as many interpretations and styles as there are mini-brads at the Making Memories warehouse.

In the end, we are storytellers. We are historians. We are documentarians. We get this incredibly unpredictable and unpolished script to work with: life. Sometimes it directs us. Sometimes it's the other way around. But mostly, it offers up one opportunity after another to tell a story. Or take a picture. And in turn, it releases the creative soul that resides within each of us.

And it's just plain fun. It's like being a kid again on so many levels. There's a joy we remember when we work with paper and glue; it's like finger-painting or pâpier maché, without as much mess.

I think that's why people get hooked. There's a truth that comes from putting experience under a microscope and retelling those stories and revisiting those memories. A truth that reminds us that life is pretty amazing. That experience is worth more than any material possession could ever possibly amount to. That time spent counting one's blessings is never time poorly spent.

I hope you never stop telling stories. I hope you never apologize for being a scrapbooker. I hope you share your pages with those you love and it reminds you of how blessed and lucky you are in this grand scheme.

I hope you continue to save the bits and pieces of your amazing, ordinary, stressed out, happy, exhilarating, unique, insert-any-other-adjective-you-like-here life.

And I hope you had fun reading this.

Go on now...go make a layout and have some fun. Keep it simple. Spread the love.

REMEMBER

LIVE YOUR LIFE FIRST. SCRAPBOOK IT SECOND. OR THIRD. OR FOURTH. DON'T BE SO FOCUSED ON THE SUPER HUGE THINGS THAT YOU OVERLOOK ALL THE AMAZING LITTLE THINGS. PHOTOS ARE NICE. STORIES ARE BETTER. DON'T TRY TO RE-INVENT THE WHEEL EVERY TIME. JUST ROTATE THE TIRES AND ENJOY THE RIDE. CREATE FOR YOURSELF. THE REST WILL FOLLOW. KEEP PAGES ON YOUR TABLE. ADMIRE THEM OFTEN. USE THE STUFF YOU LOVE. MAKE NO APOLOGIES FOR BEING YOU. FOCUS ON THE COULDS, NOT THE SHOULDS. REMEMBER THE VALUE OF WHAT YOU'RE DOING. PLAY WITH PAPER, PLAY WITH GLUE. BE BLISSFULLY BEHIND. ENJOY THE PROCESS. YOU ARE A SCRAPBOOKER. IT'S ALL GOOD.

it's NOT ABOUT THE PHOTOS

stuff I'm recommending

ONLINE RESOURCES

bigpicturescrapbooking.com

An online extension of Stacy Julian's best-selling book, *The Big Picture*, this website offers online education and inspiration.

shimelle.com

Scrapbook artist Shimelle Laine sees you through projects in your own style, from simple mini-books to collaged art journals. See box? Step outside. Remember?

twopeasinabucket.com

A great online community and store. Their talented design team, the Garden Girls, provide monthly ideas and inspiration. It's like getting an idea book online every month. Plus, I met all my scrapbooking friends here, back in the day.

simplescrapbooksmag.com

The web site for *Simple Scrapbooks* magazine. Lots of online extras, contests, and scrapbooking ideas. Want to learn more about getting simple? Then join in!

cathyzielske.typepad.com

My blog. Come on over. Hang out. Sometimes, I even talk about scrapbooking. But mostly, I talk about nothing and have fun doing it.

SCRAPBOOKING BOOKS TO READ

The Big Picture: Scrapbooking Your Life and a Whole Lot More *by Stacy Julian*

If you read only one book on scrapbooking, this is the one fully worth the price of admission! It will change the way you look at why you do this hobby and what it all means. Bottom line: Stacy Julian is a scrapbooking visionary with a message. It might just change your life.

A Designer's Eye for Scrapbooking *by Ali Edwards*

Ali strips away designer jargon and presents graphic design principles in a way that makes sense. It's enlightening to see what she chooses to document and how she does it. Her approach is ultimately real and inspiring.

Yes, It's a Scrapbook Series *by Donna Downey*

In her three-book series, Donna Downey, fabulous babe and creative genius, walks you step-by-step through a series of projects, showing you that being clever and creative can also be simple. I never knew I could cover chipboard and make a hand-bound album. Now, thanks to Donna, I do.

NON-SCRAPBOOK RELATED READING

Encyclopedia of an Ordinary Life

by Amy Krouse Rosenthal

Read this book, and in between laughing, you will be inspired to think differently about how you document your own life.

ORGANIZATION

MemoryDock

memorydock.com

This new line of photo organization and planning is just too slick for words. MemoryDock also makes a creative planner, with sections customized for scrapbookers. Whether you're planning your next layout or your next meal, this system has everything to keep you on track and creatively organized.

BLOG SERVICES

typepad.com

blogger.com

Don't be afraid to jump on the blog bandwagon. It's fun, easy and will get you writing more.

MOVIES AND MUSIC

The Shawshank Redemption

No, this isn't scrapbook related, but this movie moves my soul. I love a good chick flick that masquerades as a prison movie.

Green Day and Foo Fighters

Can you say, "I'm 40 and I rock!"? I can, and I do. I'm not saying you have to listen to these bands, but whatever you do listen to while creating, or cleaning your house, or just sitting around doing nothing, make sure it's something you love.

materials index

74 | Five
metal letters (Making Memories) + Zurich font

75 | Play
patterned paper, rubber letters (Scrapworks) + Univers font

76 | Six
patterned paper, letter stickers (American Crafts) + silk flower (Heidi Swapp) + circle punch (Marvy Uchida) + circle tag + Caecilia font

77 | Minneapolis, Saint Paul
circle punch (Marvy Uchida) + foam tape (3M) + Caecilia font

78 | Me & D
patterned paper (KI Memories) + letter stickers (SEI) + stamping ink + circle punch (Marvy Uchida) + pen (Creative Memories)

79 | Nine Years Old
patterned paper, coasters (SEI) + corner rounder (Creative Memories) + Avenir font

80 | Conduct
Avenir font

81 | One Tough Hombré
Helvetica Neue font

82 | Learning Stairway
patterned paper (My Mind's Eye) + Stephanie Marie, Interstate and Times New Roman fonts

83 | Homework
letter stickers (Sticker Studio) + chipboard letter, word tile (Making Memories) + pen (EK Success)

84 | Studio Envy
patterned paper (BasicGrey) + label holder (Making Memories) + Interstate font

86 | First Day
Times font

88 | Gear
letter stickers (American Crafts) + Adobe Garamond font

88 | Rushmore
patterned paper, letter stickers (Scrapworks) + mini-brads (American Crafts) + Interstate font

89 | Silly, Goofy
patterned paper (Die Cuts With a View) + chipboard letters (Heidi Swapp) + square punch (Marvy Uchida) + pen (EK Success)

90 | Girls' Weekend
stickers (7gypsies) + Avenir font + stamping ink

91 | Leigh Anna at Four
chipboard letter, decorative tape (Heidi Swapp) + brad (American Crafts) + paint (Making Memories) + pen (EK Success) + tag punch

92 | Summertime
patterned paper (Chatterbox) + wooden flowers (Li'l Davis Designs) + Cezanne font + photos by Donna Downey

92 | Reflect
Wild Asparagus patterned paper, title die-cut (My Mind's Eye) + decorative brads, foam stamp (Making Memories) + paper flower + pen (EK Success) + stamping ink

93 | Us, Together
patterned paper, die-cut flowers (My Mind's Eye) + plastic letters (Heidi Swapp) + foam tape (3M)

94 | Rock and Roll
patterned paper (Arctic Frog) + brads (American Crafts) + Zurich and Two Peas Ballerina font

95 | I Resolve
patterned paper (My Mind's Eye) + ribbon (American Crafts) + brad, paper flower (Making Memories) + Interstate font + stamping ink

96 | Sledgehammer
Univers font

97 | My Favorite Room
Officina Sans and Adobe Garamond fonts

98 | Coleman
patterned paper (Chatterbox) + plastic letters, plastic index tab (Heidi Swapp) + Gill Sans and Onyx fonts

100 | Matt, Jake and Nick
Interstate font

101 | Connected
patterned paper (We R Memory Keepers) + Avenir font

102 | Tales of a Fourth Grade Something
patterned paper, letter sticker, brad (Making Memories) + paper flowers (Prima) + Times New Roman font

103 | Really Zielske
metal letter (Making Memories) + Avenir font

O W N S C R A P

perspective is a beautiful thing

Remember when I said I'd never made a closing page for an album? Well, I decided to try it out. So here's my closing page for this book. Some people call it an epilogue. Mine is about perspective. And I have a little story that goes like this:

One afternoon, I walked into my scrapbook/dining room, looking for some cardstock, and noticed that my scrabble words that say "scrap now" had been changed to "owns crap." My brother-in-law, Jonathan, and Dan apparently thought they'd have some fun with my, well, crap.

I thought it was brilliant. Because it's true—I do own crap. Tons and tons of it. But I make really cool stuff with all this so-called crap. I play with my memories. I record life. I preserve a sampling of this life I'm so incredibly priveleged to live. Hopefully I'll be doing it for many, many years to come.

So let's hear it for crap, and for the good stuff that comes out of it. Is there a moral to this? Yes there is. Be proud of what you create. Scrapbooking is cool. Afterall, it's not just any crap. It's yours.

about the author

Cathy Zielske was born and raised in Everett, Washington, though she often just says, "Seattle," because she thinks it sounds much hipper. She now makes her home in St. Paul, Minnesota, with her husband, Dan, and children, Aidan and Cole.

After working for many years as a graphic designer in corporate America, she left her job after the birth of her second child to freelance and savor the taste of stay-at-home-momhood.

Then, much to her surprise, she started scrapbooking.

She is also learning to play the guitar, and has been working on learning the Indigo Girls' "Closer to Fine" for several months. However, she cannot sing.

simplify.